copyright ©2022 by Michael Frantz   All Rights Reserved

No part of this publication may be reproduced, stored in a retrieval system, or transmitted in any form or by any means, electronic, mechanical, photocopying, recording, scanning, or otherwise, without either the prior written permission of the publisher. For information address the Permissions Dept., Olive Publishing, LLC, 30 N Gould St., Suite 4000, Sheridan, WY 82801: olivepublishingllc.com

Limit of Liability/Legal Disclaimer: While the publisher and author have used their best efforts in preparing this book, they make no legal or commercial representations and any information contained in this book is not intended to constitute advice or product placement. Readers should not act upon any information within this book without seeking professional help. The advice contained herein may not be suitable for your travel situations. Neither the publisher nor author shall be liable for any loss of profit, comfort, conditions or any other commercial damages, including but not limited to special, incidental, consequential, or other damages prior, during or after any travel. Remember to flush.

Edit/format/cover design by Genesis Design and Editing, LLC; Cover-art and Illustrations by James Walker.

Library of Congress Cataloging-to-Publication Data:

Frantz, Michael - Don't Travel With Mike

Michael Frantz - "An Olive Publishing, LLC book"  First U.S. Edition 2022

Includes illustrations and references to personal travel experiences1. Travel 2. Michael Frantz 3. Beginning 4. Flying 5. Hospital 6. Foreign 7. Airplanes 8. Alcohol 9. Boats 10. Bathroom 11. Lodging 12. People 13. World 14. Boom 15. Rookies 16. Wheels 17. Hunting 18. Noises 19. Finale

ISBN(s) 978-1-7364715-6-2 softcover; 978-1-7364715-7-9 eBook

https://mikefrantz.substack.com - author website
10 2 9 1 8 3 7 4 6 5

# Contents

The Beginning ........................................................................ 3

It's Rational to Be Afraid of Flying .................................... 11

The Hospitals ....................................................................... 19

Foreign Travel ...................................................................... 29

Facebook Has Its Good Side ............................................... 43

It's 5 o'clock Somewhere ..................................................... 59

Boats and Fishing ................................................................ 67

Bathroom Humor ................................................................. 83

Lodging ................................................................................. 87

People and the Stuff they Say and Do ............................... 93

It's a Big, Big, Big World Out There ................................. 97

Let's Talk About Things That Go Boom ......................... 113

The Rookies ........................................................................ 119

Things With Wheels .......................................................... 125

Four Pheasant and a Fish ................................................. 133

Noises and Things in The Air .......................................... 143

The Big Finale .................................................................... 149

# The Beginning

I know right when my life of easy travel turned to that of uneasy existence. Prior to that fateful night, I wasn't afraid of flying, of driving, or quite frankly of anything. I was 18 and I was invincible! It was that night, that fateful night, that I had high hopes of sliding safely into second base with my first, serious girlfriend. Ah, young love…

As a high school senior with my full life ahead of me, and all 96 pounds of youthfulness spread evenly across my five-foot six-inch frame, I anxiously filled the tank to my parents' Pontiac Bonneville in preparation for a night of bliss. Mom had offered her Volkswagen Rabbit, but a quick comparison of backseat space made my choice easy. First it was off to the dance, but I wasn't a dancer and that was not the night's goal.

Second, I had scored a six-pack, not abs but of the mildly alcoholic laden beer Miller Lite. I had lifted them from the home fridge in the middle of the night. I placed them on the floor mat on the passenger side, right next to my date's legs where I kept the temperature control pointed toward defrost so to keep them cool.

We left the dance and did a quick scoop of the loop of our tiny, three block downtown. Assuring her that nothing was about to be missed, we headed to the highway and made a left turn south in search of an appropriate drinking, er, I mean, parking space.

Before I was able to turn south from the four way stop, toward heaven, I saw the red and blue lights flickering directly behind me in the rear view mirror. Being nervous, young, naïve, and horny, I did what all teenagers would do—I slammed the damn car into park right at the stop sign not giving a rat's fart about the implications. With a tortured tremor I said, "Here, throw this over the bottles." The "this" I was referring to was my letterman's jacket. I lettered in golf. Do you want to discuss the differences between that and, say, wrestling for legitimacy? I had a letter jacket. Anyway, her aim was far better than that of my putter. (therein lies every pun you can imagine intended).

Mr. Police Officer sauntered up to my window and he asked me to step out of the vehicle. In the early spring air, and without the benefit of my letterman's jacket, I was nipping out. I'm sure he could see those little pinpricks through my "silk-like" shirt that was too tight and unbuttoned down to my belly button. I mean, it was the era of Miami Vice and Don Johnson. I mean, Don always made it to second base. It had to be the too-tight, and unbuttoned shirt style.

The police officer, seemingly ignoring my sense of hipness and style, asked, "Have you been drinking?"

Me - truthfully, "No." At least not yet, I thought.

Police Officer - "You swerved out of your lane."

Me - nervously pointing my thumb toward the interior of the car, "Um, I guess she was sitting a little too close and, maybe, I wasn't paying enough attention?"

Police Officer - "Hmmm," then he took out his flashlight for an inspection of my parent's "high class" make out machine. The love mobile. His search found nothing but a properly dressed young lady who unsuspiciously rested her legs atop my jacket with nothing to be seen hiding underneath. He was looking at her legs, but my eyes had been looking just a bit higher for a few hours.

To this point, I was as innocent as they come. The potential minor in possession charge notwithstanding. The Police Officer figured the same and let us go with an admonition to keep our nooky out of the four lanes. I smiled and quickly agreed, and we slowly headed for the country roads.

For those not familiar with the landscape of rural Iowa, you get one paved road for every four gravel roads. Each one is a mile apart from the other on a square grid. Except not every gravel road is really gravel. Also, early springtime in Iowa makes non-paved roads rather unpredictable. In other words, they can be soggy and soft from the defrosting snow. Yet, as already alluded to, my mind was on higher level matters so my attention to that detail was a bit sub-par.

I didn't see the "Minimum Maintenance Road" sign reminding me that they don't plow this soggy sucker in the winter. Hell no. However, it looked like a nice, secluded spot and well away from Mr. Police Officer. Besides, it was sort of close to her home so it would be easy for us to stay there until two or three minutes before her curfew where I would then walk her to her front door, shake her hand, and say goodnight to her father, maintaining my promise to have her home on time and not in the family way.

One hundred yards down the pathway to my dreams we encountered a snow drift. "Aw, shucks," I said out loud. But the voices in my head said something entirely else. I smiled at my date and smoothly put the car in reverse. Lightly tapping the gas, I dropped the Bonneville to her axles in soil with a spray that would make me the envy of mud wrestlers everywhere.

Oh, man. What to do now? Ok, remain calm. Should we just crawl in the backseat anyway? Maybe I should ask her to get out and push?

I blurted to her, "Throw the beers as far ahead of the car as you can," and be still my aching heart and liver, "Let's go to your neighbors for help. They might be awake."

They weren't but we woke them up anyway. Soon, a tractor appeared. I produced this fancy, stretchy, cord-like thingy from the trunk that my dad put in for just such an occasion. The friendly neighbor hooked it all up to the car. He then backed up his tractor and snapped that sucker right in half. Fortunately, not harming any humans or vehicles in the process. We quickly packed it up and threw it toward the beers. Lucky for us, he had something of the steel can variety. The neighbor gave enough for us to get some traction. So, out we came from the mud and on our way we went. We were assuming that the neighbors would never talk to the other neighbors.

My date got home with the aforementioned handshake; no need to mention first or second base because I'd struck out on three called strikes. I schlepped myself back home, scattering mud the entire way. I parked in the street vowing to rise early to take it to the carwash. Why didn't I take it to the 24-hour carwash that night? Never mind, you wouldn't understand.

I did get up early and I cleaned that car within an ounce of its life. The problem was that dad got up earlier than I and took the Volkswagen to breakfast. He was getting away just in order to see what would become of his ride upon his return.

"Why was the car so dirty?" he asked, defying his promise never to ask a question to which the answer was something he didn't want to hear.

"Um, I took a wrong turn last night taking my date home, but as you can see, I got her cleaned up really well."

"What about the beer bottle on the passenger side?"

"Uh, beer bottle?"

"The only one left from the six-pack you took from the fridge two nights ago."

"Uh, I have no idea what you're talking about?"

"I'll take the car keys now and for quite some time."

I got nothing. Busted right down to my tighty-whitey skivvies. And, I've been punished ever since.

See, you don't want to travel with me. If you see me on the road or in an airport, just change your plans and go in the opposite direction. Don't believe me, read on....

# It's Rational to Be Afraid of Flying

I can hear you all right now, "Flying is safer than driving." Thousands? There is an average of 115,000 flights across the globe each day and you rarely ever hear of a crash. But you hear or can read about car deaths every day. So, just sit back, relax and enjoy your flight. Watch a movie, take a nap, have a drink. You know, all of those things that are frowned upon when driving.

But then I have evidence to the contrary:


Exhibit One:

I had just finished a job interview near Dekalb, Illinois. I figured it would be a good idea to take a short flight from there over to Cedar Rapids, Iowa to see my parents since I was "in the neighborhood" and over 1000 miles away from my then-home. When I write Dekalb and Cedar Rapids airports, I'm fairly certain it conjures up images of AirBusses, or at least 777's.

There I sat in the very front row. However, don't think of first class, at all, because this little plane didn't even have a bathroom. Next to me was a lovely lady near my thirtysomething age. We chatted amiably as they told us to buckle up and hang on to our asses. Well, buckle up anyway, nothing about my ass or yours, and to remember not to worry if the airbag doesn't fully inflate.

As the flight crew prepared to push back, the pilot, who had earned his driver's license only about a week before yet somehow got his flying license, came over the loudspeaker to inform us that there were thunderstorms in the area, but, "Don't worry, we have onboard radar." For some reason when he said, "Don't worry" everyone began to worry.

We weren't in the air even fifteen minutes when there was nearby lightning viewable outside windows on the left and the right. Perhaps you remember those paddles with a rubber ball and elastic band stapled to it? Those storms ping ponged us back and forth for seventeen lifetimes. Mr. I've got Onboard Radar ruined my opinion of pilots for life. I won't even get into the "Don't worry" bit.

I was resuscitated a little later and found myself holding the hand of the lady next to me. She startled, looked at our joined hands, and grew embarrassed, "I'm very sorry, I hope you didn't mind, but that was scary."

I responded, "Oh, No, that's fine." Truth be told, I have no idea who initiated the hand holding, but it seemingly saved my life.

Exhibit Two:

I once rode a hotel shuttle from the airport with the flight crew after we'd had a particularly jolting landing.

Pilot One, "It wasn't the pilot's fault."

Flight Attendant One, "It wasn't Air Traffic Control's fault."

Flight Attendant Two said smiling, "It was the asphalt."


Believe it or not, float planes take off and land on water more smoothly than those that use paved runways. I'm probably the calmest on float plans because where they're flown there are hundreds of bodies of water, and they can pretty much land on any of them. And we are only a few hundred to a couple thousand feet off the ground. I mean, what could go wrong? Worse case is we get stranded on a strange lake that hasn't been actively fished for decades. Winning.

Anyway, on this day, my buddy and I were taking a three-seat floater for an approximate 30-40 minute flight to prime fishing grounds. The wind speed was about 40 mph, knots, or nautical miles, whatever, but the pilot said it was a tailwind, as if that was a good thing.

When you vacation to locations that are not accessible by anything but plane or snowmobile, depending on the season, supplies will get flown in with the customers and refuse gets flown out after you've landed. So, my fishing rod holder is made of a hard plastic. A big Bazooka that is about eight feet long with a circumference of twelve inches. The interior plane space was about seven-and-a-half feet. In order for everything to fit the pilot had to fly sitting a bit twisted at a forty-five-degree angle with my Bazooka poking into his right shoulder blade causing his right butt cheek to be pushed off his seat. I'm sure the FAA would have had a problem with that, had they been there to govern the float squad.

The lodge had ordered two hundred dozen minnows to be flown in two bags. Each bag was half filled with water and the other half with oxygenated air. As I previously mentioned, the interior space was limited so I flew with one bag under each arm. From what I could see, I don't think those minnows had any idea I was about to stick a hook through them in my vain attempt to catch a lunker.

We taxied for about an hour because you have to take-off and land into the wind. The bigger the wind, the longer the necessary runway, er, waterway. Once airborne, we made the trip in fourteen minutes. How do I know? I always used to count the minutes until my certain demise with deadly accuracy. We cleared the last set of trees protecting our desired lake and the pilot made a nosedive for the water. I'm guessing we came down at an eighty-nine degree angle.

Miraculously we landed safely but we were not out of the woods yet, much less the water. That wind was blowing straight into our camp area disallowing the plane to safely coast to the sturdy docks. No, we were on the opposite side of a freaking 44,000 acre lake.

Never fear, the crusty, old lodge owner was soon seen coming to our rescue. As he neared, it was clear he was pulling a second, sixteen-foot boat, both motored by a single, whopping fifteen horse engine. Why did he have a second boat, you ask? Sane people would assume one was to carry our gear and the other our people. Instead, today was cardboard recycling day.

"Stand on the pontoons," ordered the pilot.

"What's the depth of the water?" I asked.

"Couple hundred feet."

"Good, who needs life jackets when I can easily touch the bottom?"

One bag came off, two flattened boxes went on. One off, two on. That lasted for about half an hour.

"Get in, they're only four footers," growled the owner.

I assume he meant wave size, but he could have been talking about the sharks circling the boat, too. I felt like we were about to die and become fish food. The circle of life.

Exhibit Three:

Once upon a time, and perhaps it is still this way, but I've never gone back to confirm, there were two Indian airlines: India Air and Air India. There were two distinct differences—one flew only within the country while the other flew internationally; goats and chickens were allowed to fly in the back of one while only goat and chicken herders were allowed in the back of the other.

I was riding with the livestock and part of a group of international college recruiters whose employers had each taken out heavy life insurance policies on us. If we died at least the endowments would be enriched.

Airline employees quit using the term turbulence many years ago and replaced it with "unexpected rough air." Well, we were in an unexpected Cat 4 rough air patch where we were the feather and Mother Nature was shooting us with a hair dryer. Every time we settled down to a soft, controlled descent, she hit the power button and shot back, rocketing us as we hung on by life's thinnest string.

"Are we going to die?" screamed one of my traveling companions.

I swear I didn't yell that out loud, it really was her, but that isn't to say my inner voices weren't screaming the same thing.

The goats and chickens chimed in, drowning out our indoor and outdoor voices. Good thing we were traveling in Hindu-rich India, because I was reincarnated upon landing.

Thankfully not as a goat.

# The Hospitals

The first time:

It was a nice, fall Saturday afternoon three days before I was to leave on my first professional, international trip. My neighbor and I had a little tradition of planting a cold beer can in the other's yard when one was mowing and the other, uh, just drinking. If not exploded by the mower's blades, you got a nice break from your yard work. As I recall, we were drinking Milwaukee's Best, The Beast, in those days.

Anyway, my wife and daughter were out of town for the day, so I had not yet had my friend over to watch some football. Partway through the game I heard the unmistakable sound of my neighbor's lawn mower, so I grabbed a beer from the nearby fridge, raced out to his yard, and planted his prize before racing back hoping to go unseen.

The wooden deck leading to my sliding glass back door had four measly steps. I managed to miss step number two. Perhaps I'd had too many liquid hamburgers. I threw my arms out to stop my fall and only one of them did its job. I entered my home with one arm hanging much lower than the other.

"Guess I'm going to need to go to the hospital," I told my fellow game watcher, "but I need to piss first."

After doing my business, I realized that it is impossible to button and zip your pants with only one functioning arm and that dislocating your shoulder does indeed hurt, but the pain is lessened if you hold your arm firmly against your stomach.

Before returning downstairs, I grabbed two neckties. "Please make me a sling out of these," I said to the guy who would be taking me to the hospital.

"Thanks, that feels better. Now, um, would you mind buttoning and zipping my pants?"

If looks could kill.

"I'll never tell another living soul, I promise," was all I could muster.

I'll spare you the details of the hospital with the exception that when you lived in a rural area in the 90's and your rent-an-ER-doc-on-the-weekend doesn't carry the right malpractice insurance to put your shoulder back in its proper setting, you get an ambulance ride. I'm sure it was a hoot, but a little Demerol on top of The Beast got me a very fine nap.

Back home, sling over bare skin, blanket covering sling, again watching football when the wife and daughter return with a "How was your day?"

I flung the blanket back. She says, "Oh my God, you are not going on your trip!"

"All expenses paid to Tokyo and Seoul? Are you kidding me? I'll be just fine." Somehow, the orthopedist agreed with me on Monday with the admonishment to do my rehab exercises while away.

I had my brother tie me a few ties that I could wear when needed and just cinch up, so I looked presentable in the office the day before I left overseas. Word spread quickly down the hallway to my boss who stepped into my office, "You know you don't have to go?"

"Non-refundable tickets and hotel rooms. Besides, I think I like sushi and dog meat."

One-armed I drove to the airport. I had one of those nice aluminum, rolling, pull cart things upon which to transport my baggage. It made it halfway to the ticket agent before bending in half and snapping in two.

That was a fun trip.

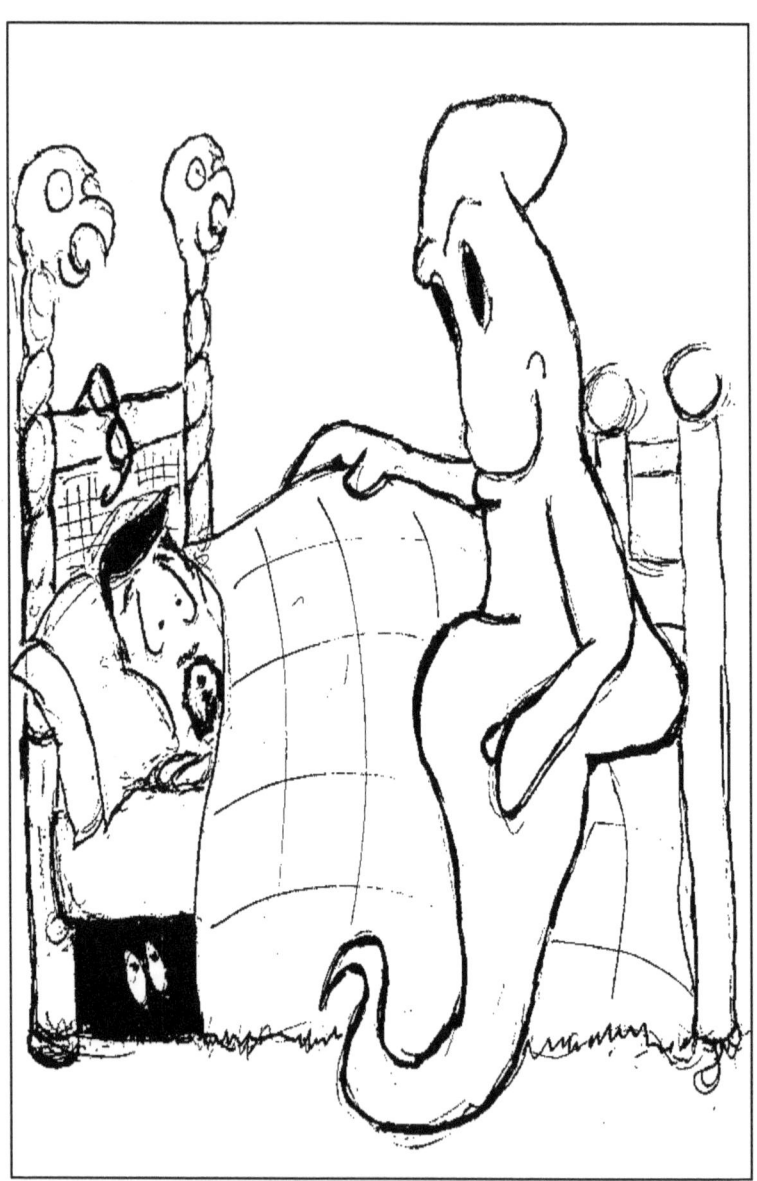

The second time:

The Adirondacks are beautiful.

I had a consulting client in its wilderness over several years and I saw it in all its glory. On that day it was a chilly -21F degrees. That's a real temperature and people were frozen in their tracks waiting to be stacked like cordwood until spring. The fall season is one where I almost crashed the car because the colors were impossible not to be ignored. Then, in the summer when the black flies gently kissed my skin with the fangs of a vampire.

This was a gloomy November. I headed north on the thruway or Northway or whatever term the locals used for the interstate that headed to Canada. As I neared Glen Falls, it began to rain, sleet, and freeze so I did what every responsible adult would do. I pulled into the rest stop to see if the roads were becoming icy. And, I had to pee anyway. Which was icy too.

I'd done another smart thing and rented a four-wheel drive tank of an SUV for the trip, just in case. It didn't matter that I needed a ladder to climb into the driver's seat.

I eased into the designated parking area for cars, carefully climbed down and alit onto the ground still wearing my work clothes including tractionless work shoes. I put one foot on the sidewalk and sat down. Okay, I fell down, as in up to the legs, down go the hands to break the impending collision with concrete. Then, shoulder number two decides to join its brother in dislocation land. Good thing I got off the road because it could have been a car wreck instead.

I still had to pee but forgot lesson number one about dislocated shoulders. I imagine that the hospital staff had seen tighty whities before. I crawled back into the vehicle to stay warm and called 911. Then I called my wife. Because going into shock all alone, in upstate New York, is not anyone's dream.

Maybe I should have called someone else because that needlessly worried her. Soon enough I was in good hands in another ER. After the necessary x-rays and clicking and clucking of nurses and doctors, I finally asked for some ice packs to dull the pain. The not-a-rent-a-doc said, "Hang in there, the Demerol is coming."

"Nonetheless, I wouldn't mind some ice packs. And, have you done this thing before?" I asked hesitantly trying not to sound like an ass.

"Honey, you're in ski country. We have lots of practice." That made sense.

I got my ice and my drugs. Right before I went to talk with the angels, I saw them wrapping a sheet around my arm. One guy who either had done serious time and/or was an ex-NFL lineman was holding my body while two WWE heavyweights were wrapping the sheet around their telephone pole like forearms.

Good night world.

When I came to, I was on a gurney in a hallway with a warm, no longer ice, pack between my legs. I had peed at the rest stop so that answered one of my questions. I was hooked up to an IV and monitor. I waited patiently for an hour. Well, maybe two minutes. And no one came by to check on me. So, I unclipped the technical doohickey that is meant to measure my brain activity or heartbeat, or some sort of life saving monitor. The machine made lots of unwelcome noises. And, again, for another hour, no one checked on me.

When the angel of mercy finally appeared, I said I was ready to leave. She said that the doctor had to release me, and we had a debate about patient rights. She was quick with her retorts. I won by telling her that I would remove the IV myself or else. One hundred dollars of a co-pay later and a couple signatures promising that I wouldn't sue the doctor who wouldn't release me, and I called a cab.

Only a few hours later I called the same cab back to take me to the rest stop where I found my mountain climber capable SUV covered in a half inch of ice. Being familiar with winter in the north, I turned the defrost on high. I'm sure if I'd waited until, say, May, it would have melted. Instead, because it didn't come equipped with the necessary ice chipping apparatus, I wielded my ballpoint pen. I eagerly got to work with my coat draped over my shoulders and one arm in the sling.

All in all, I was only an hour late to my consulting gig. Which I delivered in the obligatory green hospital top.

Yeah, they had to cut my shirt off of me, but at least they saved my tie.

Man, I miss that shirt.


The third time:

Here's the bad news. When you dislocate your shoulder at a young, but not too young, age and you have had mostly sedentary jobs, they don't rush to do surgery. So, fast forward twenty or more years and that shit bites you in the…shoulder.

Yep, labrum surgery. Those small tears that went unnoticed a couple decades ago, come back with a vengeance when you're trying to pick your nose or change the radio station in your car.

But here's the good news, you learn new tricks when your right arm is in a padded sling with a stress ball attached. Why do they have gaps in most steering wheels? For poor schmucks like me who have to weave the truck key between them to the ignition slot with their left hand and turn it to fire up the engine. With a pillow under my right elbow and one hand steady on the wheel, I was that guy weaving around the rural roads trying to get to wherever I needed to get to.

And the really, really good news? Looks like a handi-capable allows you to board the plane first when they call for those customers who need extra time. If you play your cards right, you might negotiate a golf cart ride through the terminal.

And the really, really, really good news? Your seatmate won't try to crowd you at all, no matter how fat they are, because they are scared of bumping your arm and you crying out in pain and then threatening to sue them for extreme bodily injury. I milked that sucker for months and I've yet to throw away the padded sling just in case I might need more seat room on a future flight.

It fits nicely in my carry-on.

# Foreign Travel

I have my own words of advice to the general public at large:

You Should Have Never Let Mike out of the Country


**Kuala Lumpur, Malaysia**

Another international recruiting trip. No plane problems, just people problems. We hooked up with a bunch of young entrepreneurs who were intent on killing our livers and taking our money.

At some point in the blurry evening, one of the dudes said, "Want a woman?" then made the universal hand signal indicating heterosexual intercourse, just in case his English wasn't quite good enough.

I replied, "No thank you."

"Oh," he says, "you want girl-boy?" then made the universal hand signal indicating male homosexual intercourse.

Again, I replied, "No thank you."

Finally, they took me back to my hotel where I undressed down to my skivvies and climbed into bed (alone). The bedside phone rang just as I turned out the lights.

"Hello?"

"Mr. Mike, Mr. Mike, want any woman?" Fortunately, I could not see any hand signals.

I hung up the phone with a grunt.

They were young, entrepreneurial and I'd seen the native Malay women (gorgeous if you must ask) on the arms of too many old, fat, sweaty, white, American men to understand the game at play.

The phone rang again, and I unplugged it. Sweet dreams, Mr. Mike.

Somewhere in East Germany

Study abroad back before Mr. Gorbachev took down the wall at President Reagan's request. We took the overnight train into and back out of the divided country and, I must still say, those tracks sucked. We rolled and twisted and bumped through the desolation.

But the reward was a few days in free Berlin. The liquid bratwurst flowed like it was 1999, though it was only 1985. I met up with my cousin (truth, though unnamed) who was living there and subsisting on dishwashing and dealing. I scored some prime hash. We took a few freebie hits, then met my group for a boat ride on a lake in the city. At least, I think it was on a lake, but it could have been the ocean or the Iowa River. Hard to say when you're high.

Finally, it was time for the train ride out through East Germany. Young, dumb, and not fearing a communist prison, I stuck the hash in the pillowcase of my train bunk and went to sleep. I slept hard until an SS officer, or maybe he was KGB or Interpol or just a poor teenager doing mandatory military service, rattled me awake, "Fahrkarte, bitte!" You've seen the Indian Jones movie where the same line was used so you don't need a translation about him wanting to see my ticket.

I shoved it at him and went back to sleep. "Passport, bitte!" he shouted.

"Piss (or insert profane word here) off," I responded.

"PASSPORT, BITTE!!!!" roused me again.

I shoved it up his nose or handed it to him, it was hard to say. I went back to sleep, being young, hungover, and coming down off a high.

He tweaked my nose with my passport to compare my stupid face with the stupid passport picture. I went back to sleep while he stamped his papers, picked his nose, called the Fuhrer, or whatever the commies did back then. Then, he tweaked my nose again to hand back my passport out of his hell's kitchen of a grasp. Their beer and soda pop sucked, and I was happy to leave.

It was only a decade or two later that I realized I could have ended up in their version of a Turkish prison. Glad I was naïve.

That hash ran out but my then girlfriend sent me a joint through the normal international mail service where it fell out of a lovely "I MISS YOU" card during class. Oops. A stateside friend sent me some more hash simply taped to a letter with masking tape. I was a hero among my co-ed friends. A stupid one, but a hero, nonetheless.

Are you ready to travel with Mike yet?


Vienna, Austria

We were walking through Stephansplatz, the big pedestrian zone in the heart of Vienna after a few too many liquid wienerschnitzels when a car drove by.

Me being me shouted something to the effect of "What are you kind sirs doing driving on my sidewalk?"

Said kind sirs were the Polizei (even you can translate that). They inquired as to my mental state. I couldn't blame them.

I responded that I would soon be going to bed and thereafter leaving their country forever.

Another jail term averted.

Dhaka, Bangladesh

Yep, more international student recruiting. The skies were friendly, and we landed without incident to be met by the prearranged van driver for the trip from the airport to the hotel. He informed us that there was a nationwide strike demanding brown rice instead of white or red beans instead of brown. I kind of understood where he was coming from.

He expounded, a nationwide strike meant no one could work and the simple fact that he was working by driving us put us all at extreme risk. I mean, they might throw dirty old socks at us or even a ten-day old, dead chicken. Then, the gun arrived.

Along with the guy carrying it. He might have been military, Boy Scouts International, black ops, or, even Blackwater. I quit asking questions as he sat in the middle of the van aisle pointing the gun at the ceiling as if parachuters were about to land. I almost asked, "Shouldn't you be pointing that out the window to ward off strikers?" But I was sober for once and kept my mouth shut.

I survived to write about it.


Every Airport in India

I'm glad I was trained in Bangladesh regarding guns. In India, you don't just check your bags once, but twice. You do it the usual way the first time then wait for hours in a terminal that looks a lot like airport hangars in the rest of the world until someone makes an announcement you don't understand but the natives all stand up and head for the door to the tarmac.

Sitting on said tarmac is everyone's luggage, minus the chickens and goats who have already cleared airport security and are waiting for you to pet them in the back of the plane. Alongside your luggage are military looking people with guns that were found during WWI in the fjords of Norway. I'm sure they weren't accurate but even I wasn't dumb enough to put that to the test.

Under their watchful supervision, each passenger had to touch each piece of luggage and claim it as their own before being allowed to board. I have no freaking idea how they kept track of who pointed to what, but it didn't matter as long as the gun barrel didn't point at my front or back.

That's why I'm a pacifist.


Stuttgart, West Germany (it was West Germany in 1985 anyway)

I love my wife. I loved her before she became my wife. She told me she loved me before we had our first kiss. Of course, she wasn't in her right mind. Some might argue that is still the case having been married to me over 35 years now.

We'd been out for a night of jazz and liquid pretzels when we realized the last train to Georgia or Geratstaaten was about to leave the station. Throwing caution to the wind, we ran through the rain soaked streets, down the slippery steps into the station, and jumped on the train seconds before the doors closed.

Thanking our good fortune through the first two stops, we were slow to realize the southbound train we'd boarded was heading north. Bummer.

It's a good thing young, drunk Americans are well known and understood around the globe. We found a friendly cab driver who was only too happy to ask how much money we had and inform us that it was exactly the amount necessary for him to deliver us to our homes. You don't find honesty like that just anywhere.


Hamburg, West Germany

Still on study abroad. My family had hosted an exchange student from Bremen the prior year so when I found myself in his home country a reunion was a must.

I took the train from Stuttgart to Bremen where he met me with a beer in one hand and a cigarette in the other.

He had two buddies waiting in the car. With a smirk, he said, "We are going to Hamburg?"

I replied, "Okay, why?"

He answered, "Puffviertel."

I was relatively fluent in the German language but that was a new word, "What's that?"

"You'll see," followed by giggles from all three of them.

We arrived at the desired Puffviertel which looked and smelled a lot like the French Quarter in the heat of summer. There were nice looking, albeit scantily clad women sitting on glass enclosed porches with colored lighting bathing them in glow.

We ventured past and soon stood at the threshold of a covered alleyway. There was this white line painted on the ground marking the division between sidewalk and alley.

We stepped over the white line and were individually surrounded by the most beautiful women on the planet, all dressed in virginal white teddies. Hands (not mine) touched body parts and invitations to tea were extended. It was the most exciting, frightening time of my young life. I escaped with my morals back to the sidewalk.

The Germans were having a lot of fun at my expense. I asked them to find someplace quiet. Feeling my discomfort, they took me next to an out-of-the-way bar.

Where the first thing I saw were a bored couple having sex on the stage. Once they grew tired, two women too old for the covered alleyway or glass enclosed porches, but less dressed than their younger peers, shimmied and shook their little pectoral muscles.

Upon completion of their dance routine, they mingled with the patrons. When one looked at the menus on the tabletops one learned that a decent beer cost about $1 American. Why look at the other side of the menu where one learned (if one read German) that orange juice cost $50. These aristocratic women only wanted orange juice to revive them from the exhaustion of doing the Hokey Pokey.

The skinnier of the two saw her mark at a table next to mine and went in for the drink order. He was an aged American probably away from his wife for the first time in 53 years. I instructed him on her intent.

Never before, or since, have I been yelled at by a naked, wrinkled woman in public.

Somewhere in Western Europe

I went on one of those college-led, forty countries in thirty day "study" tours. I was sober upon arrival and upon departure.

This was before the European Union and the common currency of the Euro. Each new country meant you had to exchange your pennies for your shillings then your shillings for pfennigs and your liver for your kidneys.

Part way through the trip we ended up in some town in some country that had a bar. Said bar was occupied by countrymen around our age. I had some of the proper currency, as did the countrymen. My female traveling companions did not.

Somewhere, somehow along the way the females came to the understanding that the nice countrymen were paying for their drinks. Somewhere, somehow along the way, the nice countrymen thought that playing nice with the women would result in invitations to hotel rooms. I can't imagine how that all happened because my inebriated German was flawless.

The night drew to a close because we closed the bar. All of us were ordered onto the sidewalk where the nice countrymen awaited the promised invitations and the women started weaving their way back to the hotel without extending the anticipated invitation.

Suddenly, the bartender appeared on the sidewalk, looked left, then right, and yelled at the women that they had an open bar tab to settle. Some stupid member of our group instructed the women to run. So, they did.

You know the whole saying about being chased by a predator? You just have to run faster than the slowest among you. That bartender tackled the woman closest to his bear-like size. I have no idea what happened after that, because I crossed the street and walked the other direction, around the block back to the hotel. Screw that chivalry stuff.

We were walking the streets of Stuttgart one night for no known reason during a weekend of our study abroad experience. Walking makes me thirsty.

I spotted a kiosk that sold to-go beer and purchased a six-pack. After completing the required financial transaction, I walked away and distributed the bottles to my classmates.

We quickly noticed white sediment at the bottom of each bottle. I hot stepped them back to the kiosk assuming I had just been sold bad beer. My German was good, but my vocabulary was at Kindergarten level.

Me: Kind sir, my beer is bad.

Employee (what I heard): You are stupid American.

Employee (what he probably said): That's just an unfiltered beer and everyone thinks it tastes better that way.

Me: I want my money back.

Employee (what I heard): Listen, you idiot, you bought, drink it or throw it away, I don't care.

Employee (what he probably said): I think if you just taste it, you'll like it. Trust me.

Me: I'm not drinking beer with semen on the bottom.

Employee (what I heard): Then you are familiar with the taste.

Employee (what he probably said): Tasty, tasty.

Me: Fine, I'll drink it.

And it was good.

# Facebook Has Its Good Side

A lot of people on social media create their own brand or style. As I perused nearly thirteen years of posts, they fell into just a few categories: the Dodgers, politics, hunting, fishing, and…….travel stories. A lot of travel stories as it turns out; over 5000 words. What follows are many of the "in the moment" posts of my misadventures.

Air

Airport/Airline Employees Always, always, always treat them well. I mean, they hold your ability to enter the terminal, get on the plane, and take you to your desired destination literally in their hands and hearts. When the American government shut down, but TSA workers were forced to show up every day, I went out of my way to thank them. I still do even though the government is not shut down anymore, although I'm sure there are those who can't tell the difference.

The preface to this is that my flight was delayed, and it was going to be a late night anyway as my home is 2.5 hours from the airport. Ultimately, we were on our way with an expected arrival time around midnight:

As I conclude my business travel season for the calendar year, I add last night's tale to my volume of stories:
Flight Attendant (FA): Anything to drink?
Me: You're going to need to jack me up on coke.
FA: Oh, we need to sober you up.
Me: No, I'm sober, just a long drive ahead (I got home at 3am).

FA returns two minutes later: That was all code for a few Jacks and Cokes, right?

Me: Unfortunately not.

FA doesn't let my glass ever go dry and upon descent asks, "Want a couple for the road?"

Me: The old man's debate, stop to pee every twenty minutes or get tired?

There was a snowstorm, so a thrice hourly stop didn't seem wise. I "sobered up" on the ride home.

As will become clear as you read further, I've long been an anxious flier—some of it for good reason, but mostly not. After 9/11, I went to my physician and explained that I had to fly but it was getting to the point where I might start scaring other passengers with my anxiety. He prescribed what I now call my "flying pills." That was all twenty years before this doozy:

I sat next to a flight attendant at dinner who, without prompting, told me about a recent red emergency—the kind where oxygen masks drop from the ceiling, you fully extend the tube, put on your mask before helping others, and don't panic when the bag doesn't fully inflate. Note to flight attendants everywhere: don't tell passengers who take anxiety meds for flying that red emergencies really happen. Geez, I thought what happened to poor Payne Stewart was just a fluke.

Remember, I told you to be nice to all employees in the airline industry. That doesn't mean you can't have a little fun with them:

Next time you fly, when the flight attendant asks for your drink order, tell them you ordered yours online to make their job easier. The reactions are, uh, interesting.

Really, you should try this one. I'm sure we'll really have the opportunity to do so in the coming years, so it is highly believable. The most common answer is something like, "Hmmm, another thing they haven't told us about or trained us on," or yet more commonly, "Are you shitting me? This company?!!!" Just make sure to laugh quickly and not drag this one out because you might not get your desired drink if you play the long game.

Flight attendant, "Want something to drink?"

Me, "I'd like to see you officiate a wedding between Prosecco and orange juice."


Drinking and air travel are synonymous according to my studied calculations. I devote a whole section to it later. Where else are people willing to lay down that sort of money for booze? I can buy a case of beer outside an airport for the price of two drafts inside. So, play with that!

She was sweet, a veteran of pushing the cart up and down the aisle. Piss her off and your call button would never work. Humor her and you were treated like first class though you sat in row 63.

Flight Attendant (FA): Want a water?

Me: Is it beer flavored?

FA: No

Me: Pass
FA: Want a snack?

Me: Are they beer flavored?

FA: No
Me: Pass


FA: You want an IPA?

Me: How did you guess?

FA: I fly, and I know things.

Later…

FA: Want another?

Me: No, we are landing in 20 minutes

FA: No, not for 30

Two minutes later

FA: Here, chug it, we land in fifteen

Me: You're my hero
Flight Attendants seem to have two settings: 1) super nice and helpful; 2) super badass:

This FA was in her early years of serving the sky gods. But, experienced enough to have learned that the airlines are big business, and she was but a gnat on its elephantine rump.

Me: You are double fisting your phones like a boss.
FA: Yep, one for me and one for the 'hos.
So began the start to a lively trip as she strutted down the middle (and only) aisle.

This one had purchased every life hack found in Flight Attendant's Monthly. The luggage, the food containers, the hand lotion, etc.

Me: Are you wearing a body cam?
FA: No, it's a fan but it helps that people think it's a body cam these days.


Apparently, there was a fight between employees in my airport bar/restaurant's back, unseen room. Said altercation put the staff into a tizzy. A supervisor was called.

When the 16 year-old manager arrived, he stood outside the kitchen doors for minutes, presumably counting his testicles. The staff implored him to call 911, which he did before entering the fight zone.

Nearly ten minutes passed before the officer of the law arrived. The manager emerged and said law enforcement was no longer necessary.

I commented to the bartender, "I'm sure the fight will get someone fired."

Bartender, "Not here."

Welcome to Detroit people, where it is not for the weak hearted. Bring your brass knuckles. On second thought, those will be confiscated, just bring those boxing gloves.

As mask regulations came into vogue some employees and some passengers took them more seriously than others. I mean, before all of this you would not have guessed so many adults had no idea where their nose was in relation to their mouth. We were at the early part of the flight where the drink cart had just emerged. I was toward the front of the plane and had already figured out the flight attendant was the type who took all regulations to the limit.

She peered down the aisle and shouted, "Hey, you, get your mask on!!!!!!!!!"
The dad sitting next to his teenage-"ish" daughter yelled back in a fuller throat, "We have a nosebleed ma'am!!!!!!!!!!"

Full blown hazmat emergency ensued. The drink cart was shoved aside amid groans of those jonesing for a drink, rubber gloves came out of nowhere to land on her hands, and armfuls of gauze were quickstepped to the poor lass. From that point forward, the flight attendant turned into sunshine and unicorns.


Seatmate (SM) on my flight upon learning I have a home insurance claim filed:
SM: Who's your agent or agency?

Me: Um, it's this national company

SM: Oh, they're awful, I own several insurance agencies, let me find you a better one.

Me: Well, I think I have to use the current one thru this claim


Upon learning I like to fish:

SM: My son runs a charter out of Jersey. Only costs 10k for 26 hours of offshore fishing. He has some big name clients, including the mob.

Me: I can catch walleye off the dock

SM: He's worth every penny

Me: Is that his price if he doesn't dispose of any bodies on the trip?

Upon removing her mask without need to eat or drink:

SM: Do you mind? This is irritating (it was a 70 minute flight, and she was two wines in already)

Me: Not at all, my dad died of Covid


When the feds dropped the mask mandate only about 10% of the passengers were still wearing them. Of those, about half still couldn't figure out how to cover their noses.


Travel tip: Don't walk through the metal detector with hands clasped in front of you. Apparently, it's the international sign that you are hiding something.


After showing my driver's license to the attending TSA official and being allowed further scrutiny, I passed through the CT scan machine thingy before coming safely out the other side before putting my license in my pocket. It was an automatic reflex thing that didn't even register with any cell in my brain.

The TSA agent was on his A-game and asked, "What did you just put in your pocket?"

I answered as honestly as I knew how, "Nothing."

"But I saw you."

I patted my pockets and felt the license. Slowly, very slowly, I reached in and removed it with just two fingers and sheepishly said, "My fault."


I can't tell you how many times I've been selected for the random search. So many that the last time, I told them to change the name on my license to "Random Search" so that it felt more personal.


The flight attendant announced that failure to comply with rules would lead to a coffee pot beating followed by her sitting on us. Think I will obey. (I told you they had only two attitudinal settings; in this case she exhibited both at once.)


The TSA took my tray off the belt to show the rest of the line the proper way to arrange your items. Alas, no upgrade or gold star for my efforts. (See, I'm a good boy to whom bad things usually happen.)

Wow, the TSA strip searched my calculator. Must be a training day at the airport.

Omaha traded half their TSA roster to New York for players to be named later. Pre-check lost every advantage it thought it had gained.

In the early days of TSA's existence, back when I was younger and dumber, we were passing through security when my wife was pulled aside to have her makeup bag examined. I showed my full ignorance by exclaiming, "Sure, like she's going to hide a bomb with her lipstick."

A well-trained officer of airport law responded, "You have two choices, shut the hell up or be subject to a cavity search."

Let's just say I didn't choose the cavity search.

During a bit of turbulence, the young girl asks her mother, "What happened to the world?"

I almost answered, but the response would have been longer than the remaining flight time.

Gate agent, "If you are flexible and want to make some money, please see me." Judging by the line of seemingly unattached young men quickly in line at the podium, one could call her good looking, but I have no knowledge of her flexibility.

My boarding pass made the machine beep. I said to the gate agent, "I guess it doesn't like me."
Gate agent: "They will like you even less in Detroit."

Gate agent, "If you look outside at the left wing of your aircraft, you'll see maintenance applying epoxy to the spot where the baggage cart accidentally hit it. It will take an hour for the epoxy to cure. We apologize for the delay."
I popped a pill while wondering if baling wire and duct tape might have been better solutions.

Ninety-year-old professor of astrophysics still working at a university, as we sat at the airport bar, "I told my minister, 'Goddammit, we need to pay more attention to the second commandment than the second amendment'; he agreed with me, except for the part of using God's name in vain."
Further conversation, "My university has tried to fire me a couple of times, so I just publish another article and tell them to go fuck themselves." Followed by slamming his shot down his throat, the glass on the counter and strutting to his gate.

Young boy to his younger brother as they walk the narrow aisle, "No! You can't just randomly pick your seat."


My DoorDash order included the hotel address and room number. I asked for contactless delivery. So, I got a picture of my delivery from OUTSIDE the entrance to the hotel. Yeah, it was 16 degrees.


Things the Flying Karen learned today:
1. Taking booze out of the restricted area and into general population causes a TSA alert.
2. Leaving your bags unattended while you return to the drinking area causes a TSA alert.
3. Failing to return to security, after repeated announcements to claim your lost credit card causes the rest of us to smile to ourselves.
4. Being that drunk before noon is unbecoming, even if the Bengals won.
5. Those tiger striped panties you keep showing off to the terminal inhabitants gave your football allegiance away.


A thirty-something man approached me as I cleared the secure area in the terminal and entered the space where passengers could be met. I had my winter coat draped over my shoulders with my white dress shirt and black pants clearly visible. I was carrying my computer bag in my right arm. My padded, slinged, left arm was noticeable.

He said, You're with the TSA, right?

Had I been on my game, my response should have been…

I'm waiting at my gate with a seat just feet from the area where TSA inspects bags that made their foreheads wrinkle. Full water bottles, 24-ounce face cream containers, and pocketknives all went in the trash. Then, they pulled a pilot over.

Pilot: I know what you're looking for. It's in that pocket, no, the other pocket.

TSA holds up a bottle opener.

Pilot: No, that's not what you're looking for, dig deeper.

Now this pocket wasn't that big, but I guess the TSA's hands were that small because he dug and dug to no avail.

Pilot: It's a Leatherman (think Swiss Army knife without the knives; a multi-purpose tool).

TSA upon finding the Leatherman: No, can't fly with this, illegal.

Pilot: It is TSA approved.

TSA: Illegal.

Pilot: Trust me, I fly for a living.

TSA: Supervisor, please.

Supervisor: Yeah, it's fine.

As I waited for a delayed flight in Detroit late one dark and stormy night, a young lass of about three or four years did her version of a gymnastics routine between the rows of seats. It didn't take long for her white pants to turn black from the carpet that I'm sure had been cleaned during the Reagan administration.

Yeah, I slept on that carpet that night. I think I've overnighted in five different airports in my life. The rates are good, in fact I heard that some people have made airport terminals their official residences. My aching body parts won't allow that, but each mortgage payment makes me want to reconsider my choices.

# It's 5 o'clock Somewhere

I've been in a lot of airports and if there is one place to always go that is packed, head to the bar. Seven o'clock in the morning, bloody Mary's flow like lava down a volcano. By mid-morning, there are no rules regarding morning, afternoon, or evening drinking. I guess you have to be drunk to rationalize paying those prices (which I happily do).

Don't think I'm a drunk. I have to drive after the end of nearly every plane trip and I've never had a DUI. But I do like me a drink or two along the way. Read on....

Flight attendant Sasha set the Row 6 record for having a beer in my hand 13 minutes after takeoff. For context, the all-time record is 10 minutes from seat 1A, set by LaTisha. After years of study, I've concluded the key is pre-flight preparation.

I do tend to have my own drinking rules; however, if the flight is in the morning, I'll go for the mimosa instead of beer. I've had that mimosa in its virginal state, with sparkling wine, and prosecco. Never with the good stuff. Usually, it comes already prepared by the flight attendant, but not always:

The bad news, when flying with the commoners, is you have to mix your own drink. The good news is they give you the whole bottle. My flying companions saw my drink and raised me four vodkas for that one-hour flight. I guess he didn't have to drive upon landing.

Really, I'm not a beer snob, but....

Dude on the barstool sitting next to me: I can't decide if this is a good beer or not.
Me: You ordered a Bud Light. Trust me, it sucks.
Dude: No, really, I think I like it.
Me: Check please!
Thank you, airlines, for your endless delays. You give me fodder for my fans.

This stuff happens all over the world. When in Ireland, you'll see a line of taps leading to wonderful beers, all carefully brewed, then Coors Light. Trust me, go over and see for yourself. The picture below illustrates this in the good 'ol US of A. Hamm's? Really? My dad used to drink that swill. It was so bad I wouldn't even boost it from the fridge to give to my enemies:

This was a first for me, in any kind of bar or restaurant. Check out the receipt on the next page.

It's not that the kitchen staff doesn't deserve a beer but it's not yet noon. No, the $3 wasn't for 60% of a beer; instead, an unrelated tip. How do they get a $5 beer and mine cost $10.49?

3.00

Thank you for dining with us!

BUY THE KITCHEN A BEER!

$5  $5  $5

www.RipnUoff.com

Guy orders two double gin and tonics at the airport and places a twenty on the bar. Bartender says, "That will be $30.28." Guys eyes widen. I am not the guy, but I've been that guy.


How not to sell booze to a traveler:
Me: Is the Catawba IPA good?
Waiter: I don't know, I don't like IPA's.
We will call this strike one.
(To be fair to the brewer, even though the waiter wouldn't have liked it, I did.)


When possible, I try to make friends with bartenders, especially if I frequent a certain airport bar with regularity. Sure, I might get a free drink here or there, but more importantly, I get someone I can talk to during lonely travel days. Everyone flies with earbuds or earphones these days, then add the masking requirements and plane conversations are at an all-time low. I've made a couple of good friends in the process.


Take Jill who slings martinis in this quaint little joint at the front end of a small terminal at Bradley International Airport in Hartford, CT. In the early days (and I was there from almost the beginning), their beer was stored in an ice-filled cooler before advancing to real taps. I guess they quickly learned that you can't make a profit on martinis alone.

Jill was in her early thirties, medium length dark hair, good looking, curves in all the right places, smart, funny, good conversationalist. I learned all of this quickly, but what follows happened during our introductory meeting.

Jill's eyes were darting from me to the only other patron like she was watching a tennis match between us when I stepped across the threshold into her establishment. She sort of nodded me to my seat as the other person began his version of loud flirting with slurred words. Now I understood what was going on.

As did the state troopers who soon arrived. As they escorted him away from what became my home away from home, he threw accusations of bias against his Polish heritage at the troopers.

You'll assume that they led him to the pokey. Oh, to the contrary, they led him to his gate. I felt bad for the flight attendants.

Oh, if you are in Terminal A in Detroit, head to the bar at the Texas Longhorn restaurant and give my regards to Jenny. If she isn't there, go to the Sushi bar and ask for the Vietnamese waitress whose name I unfortunately can neither spell nor pronounce who has a degree in sass.

After two hours sitting on the tarmac, they served drinks. At row 5, they quit service. Thank you booking agents because that $7 beer for me in row 4 never tasted so good.

This beauty is not doctor recommended (and please don't share with my doctor because he'll cease refilling my prescription for these life-saving miracles of science.) This took place about twenty years after my first prescription:

Pharmacist: Do you ride to the airport alone?

Me: Yes.

Pharmacist: Hmm, don't take the pill until you get to the airport.

Me: I always wait to do so.

Pharmacist: When you fly, do you fly alone?

Me: Almost always.

Pharmacist: It might be better if someone was around to monitor you while you are on this pill.

Me: (What I wanted to say) "Not gonna happen and what have you been smoking?"

Me: (What I said) "I'll think about that."

Pharmacist: Don't ever drink alcohol while taking this pill.

Me: (What I wanted to say) "I've been taking these pills for over twenty years and in my experience their effect is enhanced with two beers."

Me: (What I said) "I understand."

# Boats and Fishing

Let's take a break from all the airport and alcohol stories and turn our attention to boats. They are simpler means of travel that have been around almost as long as humankind. Is there an older form of transportation?

What could go wrong with water travel?


For a special occasion my wife bought me a kayak. I self-taught myself how to drive it. It was fun. But, early on, I learned a valuable lesson.

I loaded the kayak into the bed of my truck and took it just a few blocks down to the lake where I unloaded it and carried it upon my shoulder to the lakeshore. I was just a step or two from the water's edge when I got shot. Maybe I should have been wearing boat shoes, or any shoes for that matter.

Did you know that catfish barbs are serrated? Did you know that you shouldn't put the desecrated bones of dead animals through your skin?

I said to myself, "Why shucks, this kind of ruins my day on the water." Or something like that said in a salty sailor's voice.

I sort of walk-hopped back to the truck with the kayak still upon my shoulder. Fortunately, it was my left foot so I could drive a little more freely. Back home, out the truck and step, hop, step, hop to the kitchen where my wife says, "That didn't take long."

"How about a ride to the ER?" I asked as I lifted my left foot onto the counter for inspection under better lighting.

"Are you effing kidding me?" she responded, "How in the name of all that is wrong in this world did you do that while sober?"

I love my wife so. Without further conversation, she dropped me off at the emergency room to face my fate alone. She'd seen enough.

The nurses and doctors gawked and talked, hemmed and hawed, tittered and laughed. They even started calling me "Catfish Man." Seriously. I didn't think that was very professional of them, but it was kind of funny if you weren't the subject of their ridicule. Besides, I needed them to take it out and give me a tetanus shot.


I like to fish, and I've spent enough time on boats that whatever seasickness issues I might have ever had don't appear. That isn't the case for my relatives:

I rented a salmon charter for my dad, two brothers, a nephew, and my daughter on Lake Michigan. It was a little windy, so there were some rollers. My nephew, being of the weaker stomach variety, puked minutes into the journey, but rallied to reel in the first fish, from his knees, before heading back to suffer in private.

Three more fish hit the deck in just minutes. The captain, high in his second story perch, called me up the ladder, "It's getting pretty rough, how about we head in? I won't charge you for today, you get to keep the fish and we'll come back out tomorrow."

I climbed down the ladder and conversed with the family. Brother #1 said, "The fish are biting. We're staying out here."

Up the ladder I climbed to relay the message.

Brother #1 threw up three minutes later.

We caught two more fish.

Brother #2, just before he puked said, "We have to go in."

Back up the ladder, "I know, I know, we'll pay you for today."

I was a silent, steaming brother the whole ride in. Once on land and their stomachs now flipped back to their proper positions both brothers couldn't understand my silence and egged me on like only brothers can until the cork popped, "You want to know what's wrong? Your bloody (insert other brotherly language instead) egos cost us an entire day's fishing. If we caught six in an hour today, how many do you think we could have caught in eight hours? I hope you puke for days."

When in Ireland with my wife, daughter, and daughter's college friend, the women decided they wanted to visit the Skellig Islands. Something about ancient civilization, steps from the shore to the top, history, blah, blah, blah. To convince me to go, they booked a captain who would take us and fish with me while they did the exercise thing called stair stepping.

The day was foggy and damp. It was Ireland at its most normal. We chugged away from the dock and into the gloom of gentle rollers. Gentle, as in your stomach goes up, then down, then to the left, and over to the right. Or so they told me. I was fine. Couldn't see jack, which I guess is part of the problem with seasickness in that you can't get your bearings to calm your stomach nerves.

Puke, burp, puke, burp. "We need to go home."

Another fishing trip gone awry.

Remember my favorite Canadian lake? Two days stick out in my mind.

I was partnered that day with a jovial chap my junior in age and fishing experience. He liked to captain, and I liked to concentrate on fishing. I was a better fisherman than he was a captain.

We were going about Mach 3 across the water when there was a sudden noise, then all was still and very, eerily quiet. I looked around us at the water on all sides of the boat, just as it was supposed to be. In fact, we were not near the shore. Yet, there we were, parked in the middle of the lake.

They call it "high centered." That unfortunate situation where your boat sits atop a rock. If the rock is big enough, you can get out and push yourself off. If the rock is big enough.

It wouldn't have mattered because the captain was a rather large man, and I didn't have the brawn to make that happen anyway. He wasn't getting out because there was no way I could lift him back in and if he tried, he would have capsized us.

Several minutes with the oars pushing, and the motor in reverse at a high rate of rpm, saved us from a night alone on the water.

We went to our fishing hole where we quickly tangled about 200 feet of line between the two of us. We pulled the tangled mess into the boat whereupon the captain set to the task of disassembling one line from the other. From my vantage point in the front of the boat, his tactics exhibited a lack of patience and a pair of scissors.

Finally, he produced a string that included all my gear which he promptly threw overboard assuming it was still attached to my rod and reel. I watched it all sink to the bottom. He said, "Oops." I said, "Remember the scissors and what they do?"

I haven't fished with him since.


There is a main lake, then this route through the river system into a national park. From there, it branches into three arteries. It takes forever to get up to the farthest point but it's the ends that fishermen will go to find fish...

We had a full flotilla of never sober men away from their wives for a week on this trek that included a nice shore lunch.

Afterwards, having caught too few of the desired fish, my boat partner and I took off for the main lake. As you navigate previously uncharted waters you make note in your head about landmarks, so you know where to turn and what not. That works great when the landmarks are recognizable.

That tree could be any of thousands and that rock was one of tens of thousands and that bald eagle was supposed to stay sitting on that branch all day long. Yeah, we were lost with hopes the gas would hold out.

Finally, we went to the far reaches of the bay we'd been to several times previously only now to recall this was the opening, if you went deep enough. Out we came, on our way to camp and one very angry mother of a lake. We'd been in well protected environs and had not grasped that the winds had kicked up. We did what we never did.

On went the life jackets. Of course, the smart play would have been to sit back, drain the rest of our beers and hope the weather would improve. Instead, we ventured out into the gales and six footers. My captain gunned the engine up the wave, knocked her into neutral as we hit the peak, and I hung onto my seat for dear life. Had I not, I would have gone airborne.

We paralleled the shore for days, hours, minutes, who can say? I was as scared as I've ever been and that was before we looked down on one descent and saw boulders the size of our houses beneath us. It's hard to say how close they were to the surface, but we didn't want to find out. So, we did what had to be done, we went out into deeper water and bigger waves. Talk about a sobering experience.

Upon safely returning to camp, I drank a twelve-pack faster than any college kid at a fraternity party. Suddenly, Mother Nature blew her last breath and the seas calmed to glass allowing the other, wiser boats to cruise into camp.

I'd missed out on hours of fishing and wasn't going to let the perfect evening pass without getting my time in. I fell while I was getting into the boat and broke one pole. Carry on, I say, we always have extras. I stood up to fight a fish a few minutes later and promptly fell again, breaking another pole.

It couldn't have been the beer. No, I just have bad balance.

I once owned a little fourteen-foot boat with a ten-horse motor (okay, full disclosure, it was a 9.9). I had a routine with my daughter who was four or five at the time. She'd go to the bathroom before donning her swimsuit and Little Mermaid life jacket and we'd head out for an hour of fishing time.

Three minutes into the trip, she'd complain of a full bladder and drop trow. I'd hang onto Ariel's face while my daughter would hang her bony butt over the gunwale. She'd fertilize the lake and we'd finally get down to business.

I'd hook the walleye, then hand her the pole to reel it in. I'd remove the fish from the hook; she'd feed it a bit of worm as reward then kiss its head; I'd release the fish.

One day, we decided we needed a new adventure. Mom and daughter were in the car while I drove the truck and boat. I think we did the two vehicle thing because I figured I'd want to fish longer than they did. Our destination was the Iowa Great Lakes, about an hour north of home.

All goes according to plan. The boat gets launched, we find a nice quiet spot, apply sunscreen, prepare poles, and I tell my wife to drop the anchor.

She does as asked, and the anchor races to the bottom with its rope trailing behind it. Not only was the water deeper than the anchor rope's length, the anchor rope was not tied to the boat. Guess we'll troll.

My wife was in the front of the boat and my daughter was on the middle bench holding her Disney character fishing pole which was dragging a crank bait certain to catch a whopper. Soon thereafter, the pole took flight, narrowly missed my wife's nose and lodged in the front of the boat. She looked at it as if it were a fine piece of art in a fancy museum.

"Grab the pole," I shouted. More staring followed.

I repeated my command only louder and she broke from her trance, snatched the pole, and quickly handed it to me. I confirmed that a not so small fish had taken her bait. I got my daughter in my lap where I could secure both kid and pole simultaneously and coached her through the catching process.

The reward was an eight-pound sheepshead, a rough fish like a carp, worthless to every fisherperson in the world except my daughter. It was a trophy of epic proportions that was worth taking to shore for pictures and a meal. The fish's length was two-thirds the height of the girl who caught it. Many hugs, kisses, and congratulatory gestures were made before my wife distracted her enough for me to throw the damn thing in the weeds.

Completely exhausted, the girls called it a day and I motored in to let them go. Upon arrival at the dock, I looked into the parking lot at my truck and trailer to see that a trailer tire was flat. We have a term for that: ungood.

I pulled the boat into the weeds and secured it, jacked up the trailer, removed the tire, and darted off to a repair shop. The seven-year-old employee told me, "I think the patch will hold." I went back to fishing.

Where I caught jack. No, that isn't a kind of fish, at least in Iowa. I caught bupkis, which is not related to Dick Butkus.

It was getting dark by the time I'd loaded the boat and headed for home. Halfway back, approaching the only town between me and home, the patch indeed didn't hold. As in one loud sound followed by the flapping of rubber on road, then the unmistakable noise of metal making sparks on asphalt. I managed her to the side of the road where I took everything out of the boat, including the motor, and into the bed of my truck, unhitched the boat, and fired up the truck. What a day.

Five miles down the road, a keeper of the peace thought that my day wasn't yet bad enough.

"Do you know you have a headlight out?"

"Do you know that I have one less tire on my boat trailer than I should?"

"I don't see a boat trailer."

"It's five miles north of here."

"You can't drive with one headlight."

"I caught a fish on a pole that flew four feet through the air without a body attached to it. I can do anything."

"I'm going to have to give you a ticket."

"Want to hear about my anchor?"

"Okay, I'll bump it down to a warning."


My daughter convinced me to take her on a canoe down the Susquehanna River in Pennsylvania as part of a fundraising event to save the carp, remove raw sewage, or stop the flow of acid from the runoff of mine tailings. It was an admirable cause.

The day was bright, and the temperature was right. We were part of a flotilla of canoeists, all safely clad in life jackets. It was a gay old time.

We splashed others with our oars and took incoming shots across our bow. It was a perfect day, until the dark clouds started rolling in from the west. It didn't take long before the Coast Guard, Water & Rescue, and Elmer Fudd the Organizer told us to hurry along to the landing down river.

I tried, I really tried, but I was not an experienced canoeist. And, my nine-year-old daughter was no help at all except to tell me that she was scared, and I was an idiot. Every time we approached this bridge, the front of the boat would get pushed sideways toward shore. I'd get it straightened out paddling upstream, turn back downstream and back to the shore. I'm sure if there had been cell phone video back then we'd have won on "America's Funniest Home Videos".

Except something worse happened. Elmer Fudd threw me a rope from his motorized boat that I tied to the bow of the canoe, and he pulled us to safety. While I smiled and pretended to row from the back, my daughter ducked below the hull to hide her embarrassment. I won the father of the year trophy.

Back to Canada and back to fishing. There are some big pike — over forty inches – that I've seen. We fish with big crank baits equipped with three large treble hooks. I mean, how can you miss or lose a fish with nine total hooks? Sometimes you even catch more than you expect.

One thing you learn the easy way, or the hard way is that you don't ever hold that big crank bait in one hand while trying to remove the hooks from the fish's mouth with the other. The easy way to learn is to watch your boat partner get impaled. The hard way is to get impaled yourself. I chose the hard way.

The smaller the pike the feistier they are in the boat. I had a little 24-incher in the boat. Holding my bait in one hand with the fish dangling from it, I held my needle-nosed pliers in the other. Right as my boat partner yelled, "Don't do that!" the fish thrashed.

I found myself hugging the fish to my chest while making indistinguishable noises that sounded like goats being drawn and quartered. Of particular concern was that the line was still strung to the pole which was attached to the lure which was attached by hooks to the fish and also now to my thumb.

My boat partner asked, "What would you like me to do?" Through gritted teeth I instructed him to first cut the line from the pole, then with bolt cutters the hook from the fish, and finally dispose of the fish into the water. That left me with the treble hook, having entered the knuckle of my thumb and exited next to my nail, still attached.

My boat partner, continuing his helpfulness, said, "I've watched videos on how to remove the hook."

I responded, "Give me a bag of ice and take me back to camp. I'll take my chances with the weathered, old owner." So, that's what we did. Twenty grueling minutes of bouncing over waves as I wondered if my week of fishing was now over.

I presented myself to the owner on the front steps of his home. He muttered something like, "I'm really sorry this happened, and I'd be happy to help you out." Instead, it sounded a lot more like, "You *effing* American idiot, you're interrupting my siesta."

He instructed the camp's housekeeper to put a kettle of water on the stove. Why she was in the house, while his wife was not in camp, during his siesta is a question I chose not to ask. In addition to his doctoring, it looked like I was going to need some nursing.

Before I laid my hand across the table, treble hooks pointing to the ceiling, and buried my head in my good arm, I told my fishing buddy, "Don't you dare film this."

I heard surgical instruments rattle, more mumbling from the owner, and the whistle of the kettle. After that, I felt some pressure and tugging on my thumb. Voila, he pushed the barb through the skin, crimped it down, and pulled it out. How do I know all this if I wasn't watching? My buddy filmed it.

I thought we were done now that the hook was out. I was wrong again. The owner poured boiling water into a dish and placed two tea bags in it. After a minute or two, the first tea bag was placed on my thumb. What's a first degree burn on top of a puncture wound anyway?

After a few minutes, he swapped teabags. Then, I was told to get the hell away from him with instructions not to wash my thumb for 24 hours. I was in a fishing camp so there wasn't any soap to be found anywhere anyway.

As we walked back to the boat, a mere hour after the piercing, my buddy said, "You just got teabagged."

I didn't get tetanus or an infection, though.

We were vacationing in northern Minnesota on the uniquely named Long Lake. On the second day, I took the boat out to the far end of the lake to try my luck. After almost reaching my destination of lily pads and hungry bass, the engine consumed its last drop of fuel.

What to do?

I learned this is the reason the law requires there to be an oar in the boat (not two, but one because boats are just like canoes, you know?). Huff, puff, and paddle to shore. Pull the empty gas can and take the long walk back to the lodge.

Did you know that a full gas can weighs a lot more than an empty one? My return trip to the boat took three days longer than the walk to the lodge. By that time, the fish weren't hungry, but I was famished.

I figure that boat got 100 yards to the gallon.

# Bathroom Humor

I couldn't write a book that didn't have immature, boy, bathroom stories. Except, we call them lavatories on planes. Sounds so much more sophisticated. Besides, I told you to sit on your porcelain god while reading this.

The #1 rule of bathroom usage for going #2 is to always, always check to see if there is toilet paper in the dispenser BEFORE you start your business. It is written somewhere, perhaps on a bathroom wall, that the pants-and-underwear-around-the-ankles shuffle from stall to stall in search of TP is highly frowned upon.

Yes ma'am, I'll take the bathroom seat on the 30-minute flight in exchange for first class on the 2.5 hour one.

I'm not even sure it was permissible for the person to use the bathroom because the stay seated sign was still on, yet I'm sure it was an emergency because the flight attendant had to spray the LAVATORY twice with air freshener after the passenger had done her dootie.

I barely make my flight only to find a 3-year-old in my assigned seat. So, I was given the only row 1 seat on the plane. The pilot then decides my weight would be better distributed by having my butt guard the bathroom door. Damn kids anyway.

Leg one was complete, and my daughter only got locked in the plane's bathroom once.

We were on the first flight of several over two days to visit Rwanda and I didn't even know there was a problem until it was over. As a bad father, it didn't occur to me that she'd been gone that long. Yes, I was probably drinking on top of my flying pill again.

She returned with this tale: Upon flushing and washing, she couldn't get the sliding gizmo to glide all the way, thus she was imprisoned in the lavatory. Commence yelling and the appearance of the flight attendant. Because the well-educated daughter was yelling and slamming the slider from side to side, she couldn't hear the flight attendant telling her to stop, to sit down, and to shut the hell up.

The room grew hot and stuffy, and her own anxiety took over. I'm sure they could have fixed the door upon landing, and they do equip the lavatories with oxygen bags in case of loss of cabin pressure while you're in midstream. She would have been just fine.

I don't know if my daughter finally stopped due to exhaustion or frustration, but as soon as she did, the flight attendant got out her prison keys and released her from bondage. She returned to her seat beside me red faced and asked that I buy some diapers at the next stop. I'm not sure if she's used a lavatory since.

Every time I wiped, the airport toilet auto flushed and sprayed my bottom which required another wipe which resulted in another unwelcome spray. So, the dilemmas were: air dry and miss flight or get a wet bottom and hope nobody notices.

Nothing better than popping your pants button into the toilet, er, lavatory, bowl to make the rest of your day feel better.

I did not walk in on that woman in the airplane bathroom. I'm sure she left the door unlocked for someone other than me to join the mile-high club.

# Lodging

Most travel requires lodging, be it hotel, home, Quonset hut, cabin in the haunted woods, cab of your truck, or castle. I've been in all of them and lived to write about it.

It was my first visit to a West Virginia campus near a town so large it didn't have a no-tell motel or hotel. They suggested I stay in the alumni house—a kind person might call it a travel lodge. We were so far into rural West Virginia they gave you a banjo to play for yourself at the county line.

The "Alumni House" was dark and creepy. The beds were stolen from the dorms in 1965. I found a 2" dead grasshopper on the floor of my room but at least there was toilet paper. It gives me the willies just thinking about it today.

I tell the hotel manager, "There is no hot water."

She says, "It must be a town issue."

I say, "Your hot water heater is a town issue?"

She replies, "Oh."

The 14-year-old hotel clerk called me "mate" and the 12-year-old bellboy called me "bud." I suspect that the irony of me calling them each "sir" was lost on them.


I called the front desk for a breakfast room service order form. They arrived with eight hangers and a Styrofoam ice bucket. I was happy with the ice bucket.


Back in the day, I would fill the bathroom hotel sinks with ice from their dispenser, then add store bought beer. That was before I quit caring if they knew whose company was on my credit card. Now, I just sit in the bar. Or maybe I was just cheap.


Yesterday's first hotel room had no functional heating unit. The second room had no functioning TV clicker or phone. Today's hotel room is on the 15th floor and the elevators have glass walls. With my fear of heights, I have to choose between the stairs or a fetal position up next to the elevator door.


The backstory to this one is that I was staying in a campus-owned house adjacent to their public safety office. They provided the bedding, bathroom towels, and kitchen supplies. I was responsible for cleaning and laundering.

Upon first use, I followed the directions as shown in my post below and inserted the requisite number of quarters. Hitting the start button did nothing. You'll see the frustration regarding my situation for there was no provided second set of bedding:

"The coin operated washing machine in my temporary home asks that the detergent goes in the bottom before dumping the dirty clothes atop it. Great idea until one learns said washing machine doesn't work. My wash cycle with the clothes in the shower worked great but the rinse and spin cycles are sub-par. Life is glamorous while on the road. You all know why I didn't immediately go to a laundromat."

Come to find out the next day, A) the machines don't require quarters, but nobody offered me a refund, and B) the washer and dryer were known to blow the circuit breakers with some frequency. Where was a cop, or an electrician, when I needed one?

No travel story, instead a pizza story. I ordered from the same place as last week although I changed the room number on the online form. Pizza was way overdue, so I called to inquire. It appears the crooks in my old room were more than happy to consume my ill-gotten pie. Mike is close to hangry. A new pizza is coming I am told.


Hotel Receptionist: How was your stay?

Me: Fine, but the shower lost hot water.

Her: That can't be because we fixed the boiler yesterday.

Me: Hmmmm.


Back in the home state of Iowa when I traveled intra-state a lot, I never made a hotel reservation. There was always room at the local Super 8 or Motel 6 or mom 'n pop Travelodge. It never let me down.

Then, I moved to the east coast and applied my well-honed skills of traveling without planning to the Garden State of New Jersey. I'd just finished an evening event; daylight savings time had ended thus dark had enveloped the concrete landscape that is that state. One hotel after another was booked. It was getting on toward midnight.

I pulled into a temporary housing establishment that was shady, even by my standards and asked for a room. The, uh, attendant, took one look at my white skin, suit and tie and kindly responded, "You don't want to stay here, son." To which I answered, "I wish you a lifetime of good health and wealth," and ran like hell.

The next place looked markedly better. Their parking area wasn't full, and it was well lit. I approached the desk, behind which sat a matronly woman feeling quite safe behind her bulletproof glass. I'm pretty confident she had a shotgun latched under the counter and a backup midnight special taped to her ankle, "Will that be by the hour or the night, honey?"

I took the night option, but even sleeping on top of the sheets was less than comfortable. I've made reservations ever since.

The 200+ year old, campus-owned house I stayed in in MA is purportedly haunted. The first night there I couldn't get the TV or wi-fi to work. I heard lots of strange noises and will swear something larger than a mouse walked across my mattress.

One trip, I arrived during a fierce storm. At the foot of the interior stairs was nothing but an empty bed sheet. Plus, it or something else took away the beers I left there the month prior.

But the scariest part was this episode. It was early in the Trump presidency and people were still talking about his alleged sexual harassment of women as evidenced in the Access Hollywood video. I went upstairs to find this magazine on the dresser. Every time I turned it over, it was right side up the next morning.

Just what is she grabbing? Is that even her own hand? Who the hell is the editor of Town & Country and does s/he even still have a job? I guess the ghost(s) liked it.

Me to hotel reception: It appears my room hasn't been cleaned since the last occupants left.

Reception: I'll come look.

Moments later after a quick examination of my abode for the night: Are you sure you found the room this way?

Me: Even for me it would be hard to fill two garbage cans, dirty 8 towels and mess the beds in the two minutes we've been apart.

Receptionist: Well, either you can watch me clean this room for 40 minutes or I can put you in the whirlpool suite at no extra charge.

Me: Hold my beer while I think.

# People and the Stuff they Say and Do

I give you this gem, said by a young boy to his father in an airport bathroom, "You're right, Dad, if you shake it a little more pee comes out."

I nearly fell off my toilet seat. At least that one was better than the other idiots who are talking on their phones while a dozen toilets are flushing around. What are they thinking?

Random plane seat mate: Here's a picture of a giraffe I killed.

Me: I'm not sure how I feel about that.

Him: They were starving.

Me: Here's a picture of a musky I caught and released.

Him: All the liberals in Minnesota are buying all the bear tags but not using them.

Me: Here's a picture of a walleye I caught and released in Minnesota.

Him: All the liberals in Wisconsin are protecting the bears and letting all the Indians kill all the walleye.

Me: Here's a picture of a walleye I caught and released in Wisconsin. Do you hunt grouse there?

Him: Not anymore, the wolves ate them all.

Me: Um, I have to do some work

I have seldom shown such restraint, but I didn't want to be added to his trophy wall alongside a starving giraffe.

"Man, I was so disoriented when the plane landed, maybe I shouldn't have had that last shot with my beer ... this piss is the most satisfying part of my trip so far." Things I hear while minding my own business.

From the loudspeaker in the terminal, "Would Jane Doe please return to The Love Shack to pick up your wallet." This must really be a full-service airport, I muttered to myself.

One large parent called her little two-year-old "small butt." Makes me wonder what mom is called.

They just paged "passenger Elmo" and I started giggling without anyone tickling me.

# It's a Big, Big, Big World Out There

It was my first trip to India. Let's make that my last trip to India. I love and hate that country because it's beautiful and butt ugly, fantastic and fetid, noteworthy and nauseating. Anyway, I land in Delhi and have a brief overnight before departing early the next morning for another glorious and gut-wrenching location.

I leave security and am faced with an open-air sort of environment with counters offering various services. In need of local currency, I go to the banker, who looks a lot like a twelve-year-old street urchin. I hand over three or four hundred dollars' worth of Uncle Sam's greenbacks and, in exchange, I'm given two six-inch high stacks of paper rupees, each held together by similar length of heavy-duty staples. The currency is so thin, I don't think you could use it for toilet paper.

"I guess these won't fit in my wallet," I say to myself, "and what else didn't my boss tell me?" I discreetly, as if everyone within ten kilometers couldn't see me, stick them into a bag. I didn't think to bring a staple remover with me.

The next booth I approach is for a taxi. The ten-year-old says, "See that guy waving at me in the doorway? Go with him."

I answer, "You mean the one who looks like he should be in nursery school?"

"Yes, he's a very good driver." Upon seeing his mark, the young driver says, "Follow me." He doesn't offer to carry my bags.

We walk around one building, then another, never once seeing something resembling a streetlight though it is full on dark out. Ultimately, we reach a parking lot where a group, or a gang, of his nursery school classmates are hanging out. Six or sixty of them suddenly push two head-to-head cars back and a third forward. I wonder what was wrong with the other two, since they were in the front row?

"Get in and where to?" asks my driver as he sits on a telephone book in the front seat.

I give him the hotel name and address and before I can buckle my seatbelt (are you kidding there wasn't one seatbelt in the whole glorious and God-awful country), we are flying through roads of dirt alongside which are huts and outdoor fires upon which my body is sure to be roasted. This is where I get rolled and left for dead. Maybe I can leave a note in the cab that a more fortunate passenger will find and send to my wife, so they know where to send the cadaver dogs.

For all my sarcasm, and justifiable fear, I've found that ninety-nine percent of the people are really, really good. Fortunately, I've not yet met the other one percent, except the giraffe killer. My driver got me to the hotel. As I got out with my rupee laden bags he asked, "Need a ride in the morning?"

"I do."

"Call me," he replied.

"How?" This was before cell phones were given to newborns in hospitals.

"Hotel knows. Give them my card. I'll just be sleeping over there," he said pointing into the jungle.

I enter the hotel, provide proof of my existence in the form of my passport and working credit card and am given the key to my room. I head on in. I had not seen such shag carpeting since visiting my grandparents in the 60's. I'd not felt such damp carpeting since my waterbed sprang a leak in the 80's. Let's just not try to say that it had just been freshly shampooed.

Ah, they left me a nice bowl of fresh fruit, I thought to myself as I approached a bit of healthy sustenance. Just then, an army of several thousand fruit flies thwarted my efforts to eat. So, I laid down to sleep knowing my time was short and I can put up with anything.

Then the monkeys started to have sex outside my window. I hope those were sounds of ecstasy and not pain. I hope it was consensual. I wish they'd have been quieter about it. I wish that it hadn't gone all night or at least taken a smoke break.

Like always, I made it through, went to the lobby and gave them the cab driver's card. The concierge or bellhop or keeper of the cabbies went to an outdoor microphone and called the guy's name. He was there in moments eager to take me back to where it all began. Maybe I shouldn't have given him an entire stack of rupees, but he looked like he could use some toilet paper.

It was a helluva couple of weeks there. I saw elephants, horses, goats, pigs, cobra, monkeys, cattle, and chickens, and that was just on the roads and sidewalks. I had my fill of curry and rice and curry and rice. By the last stop, I'd had enough, and they advertised hamburgers on the menu. It was an international hotel with at least 2.2 stars. Cows really aren't that sacred, are they?

I learned that it is indeed possible to throw up from your toes to your nose. And then, the other explosions came----out. In the middle of all of this my boss called around 2AM to tell me he had resigned, and he didn't want me to hear it from some random, Indian cab driver. For not the first time in my life did the idea of FML enter my mind.


Being sick is bad enough, being sick overseas, alone, and afraid is the worst. I was in Japan in another hotel after another meal of mystery meat (it wasn't beef because those damn things are sacred outside of America no matter how well they advertise Kobe steaks) when my body rebelled.

Most hotels have a binder full of helpful information. You want a massage by a fully clothed Geisha girl who is of age but will be monitored by a Buddhist monk? Do you need directions to the casino where you are guaranteed to become a millionaire? Do you think you are dying and in need of an acupuncturist? I started dialing and the poor soul who answered heard my garbled litany of distresses.

Soon, a maid appeared outside my door. She held three packets of powder in her hand. She held one up and pointed to her head, then the second and pointed to her stomach, then the third and pointed to her behind. By then, I had no idea whether the first one was for the head or the stomach. Did it matter? I had all three ailments plus a bunch of others for which there were no further powders.

She left and I consumed them all. I was better in hours. See, there are good people everywhere. I just wonder what happened to all my money and clothes during the hours I can't remember after taking all the powder. Kidding. Sort of.


My daughter studied the topic of genocide while aboard in Rwanda. That did a number on her, as you might imagine. The people were great. The topic was quite a heavy load to take. So, before she left for the Peace Corps to Armenia she asked if I'd go to Rwanda with her so she could exercise some demons, or at least prove she could come home mentally healthy. I quickly agreed.

In the Nyngwe National Forest we were almost eaten by wild animals, carnivorous birds, and insects the size of dogs. Seriously, on this walk we followed a blood trail of a bobcat or something toting his lunch or so the guide said. Really a beautiful landscape every step of the way, except the bloody parts.

This took "walk to the light" in a whole new direction. One of my daughter's must dos was the canopy walk where we had to go across three "bridges" like this suspended above the forest floor (like 107 miles above it). For those who know how much I dislike heights, I post this as evidence as to how much I love my daughter. The length of this bridge was somewhere between 1000 and 10,000 meters. About halfway across, the guide stopped and told us it would be a good place to stop to take pictures. From my place in the back of the pack, I whined, "If I have to stop, I will lay down and curl into the fetal position, You'll have to figure out how to carry me out."

Here's how to build confidence in your international guests--As I'm leaving for Taiwan, the host emails, "The good news is that Typhoon Fanapi has left Taiwan and there will be no typhoon or typhoons when you are here. Statistically speaking, it is very rare to have two or more typhoons in a week."

Just like it is rare to experience an earthquake. I was on the 404th or 44th floor of a hotel in Tokyo when the building began to sway. Dressed in only my skivvies, I wondered what might cause such a thing. Being of sober head, it occurred to me that sometimes Japan suffers from earthquakes. Hmmm, what to do?

I dressed as if caught by a jealous lover with his spouse and ran down the many flights of stairs as if being chased by the same, only he had two assault rifles, a grenade launcher, and a flame thrower. I hit the lobby gasping for breath to find that business was being conducted as usual.

Maybe I should order some of that special powder while I'm down here, I wondered. Sheepishly, I got on the elevator, hit the proper buttons, and went to sleep.

Was this my imagination or are swaying buildings that common that no one cares unless they fall down and go boom?

There is another reason I'm not going back to India. It's possible I'm not allowed to. As you've read, this was not my favorite trip, but at least I had business class seating to look forward to on the return home, or so I thought.

I checked my luggage and received my boarding passes at the ticket counter. You're thinking of a fancy desk, conveyer belts for the bags, and helpful airline employees. I was seeing a folding table, donkeys with bags strapped to their backs, and people who wanted to be anywhere else. I noted that my boarding passes had me scheduled to fly with the goat owners in the back, to which I protested.

They passed me up the chain of command with each successive person being less helpful. What started as a computer error, through the game of Mike's Travels Always Suck, ended with me having changed my ticket to secure a monetary refund. Oh, hell to the no, I will spend my daughter's inheritance before I ride in the back on an international flight.

Unfortunately, this was during the days before flying pills and Mike could get pretty angry. Ultimately, through the hazy memory of my rage, I might have signed something allowing me to fly up front in exchange for never coming back to pet the cobras again.


"Let's visit Armenia and see our daughter," said my wife.

"What could go wrong?" I answered.

As you might imagine, I had accumulated a few airline miles. As they don't expire, I save them up for special things involving my wife. Like first class tickets to and from Armenia. We traveled in luxury from Omaha to Detroit to Paris.

I might also add that my wife had broken her foot just days prior to our departure. She deserved to be pampered because cruising through airports on a kneeler is hard work. I had her wheel right up to the first-class lounge within the international terminal at Charles Fucking De Gaulle Airport where I presented the snooty receptionist in the luxury lounge our boarding passes. She handed them back, informed me that we didn't have first-class tickets to Armenia, that we commoners needed to leave her rarified air immediately, and that she needed space to snort her cheese.

Row four had to be first-class, right? Nope, the row right behind. Now, I'll admit to being overweight, but by American obesity standards, I'm almost svelte. By whatever airline we were flying on, I was sumo wrestler fat, as in I could hardly get my hips down between the armrests. I gulped down the rest of my flying pills. No amount of arguing with the gate agent or flight attendant changed my predicament.

Alas, we arrived in Armenia, hugged our daughter, and left the airport without our luggage because those French bastards were inspecting it back in Paris for fleas. Or they accidentally sent it to Guam. Or they didn't give a flying rat's bottom and went on holiday.

No big deal, I could go a day or two without clean underwear. It would be just like college again. More critical was correcting the errors in our booking so that the return flight wasn't a repeat. The customer concerns concierge was really quite helpful in informing me that this was all my fault, and I had no recourse. Knowing that my call had been recorded when I made the reservations, I politely told her to, "Pull the flipping tape if you don't believe me."

As an example of my confidence, before ending the phone call, I upgraded our return tickets to first-class and they charged $10,000 to my credit card.

The airline delivered my wife's luggage the next day and smirked at me.

On day four, I made my daughter take me clothes shopping. You've seen the pictures of Russian men on the beach with their vodka bellies hanging over their teeny weenies? Yep, the only available underwear fit me better than any Olympic swimmer. And the shirts fit me like a latex glove.

We had a lovely visit during which I got to pay for all of the meals and booze for a bunch of starving and thirsty Peace Corps volunteers. I even managed to destroy the shower chair I'd packed for my wife to assist her with her hygiene.

On the tenth day of a twelve-day trip, the kidnappers released my imprisoned clothes. Oh good, I wouldn't need to do laundry right away when we got home.

Because I was laundry duty free, I spent my time crafting an email to the airline describing their transgressions: botched booking, lost luggage, rude customer service, no offer of a wheelchair for my impaired wife, Russian underwear, etc. I threw it all at them.

In return, they sent me 100,000 miles and refunded my money. When Mike's right, he puts up a fight.

I have good reason to be scared of flying, especially the landing part. When we lived in northeastern Pennsylvania, the local airport was situated on top of a mountain they'd flattened. You didn't want to lack speed on takeoff or come up a foot short on landing.

That was good practice for Osaka, Japan where they built the landing strips out into the ocean. You know you're coming in for a landing as you look out your window and see water, water, water, touch down. I swear there is a whale out there with skid marks on its back.

The old Hong Kong airport was even better. The arriving planes literally had to tilt their wings to pass between skyscrapers. I mean, I've seen bosses boffing their secretaries and clerks playing solitaire at their desks while flying by their offices.

On our return from Rwanda, I had an extra special bonding experience with my daughter. Three days together in the Brussels' airport. Something about a broken plane part that had to be ordered from NAPA whose only delivery mechanism was a slow boat through the Panama Canal.

From my recollection, the airport had one bar and one restaurant that only sold salted pretzels. As passengers, we were told to report to the airport every morning and patiently wait for updates until they closed the airport, then rinse and repeat.

I finally managed to book us a different way home and beat the original plane by three hours. Except, they never took our luggage off the original plane, so we had to wait in the airport for the rest of those schmucks to catch up.

Then, there are the foods of the world. Lots of travelers look for the familiar golden arches and similar chains that litter the globe. Not me, I want to try new stuff.

When in Seoul, the hotel restaurant was kind enough to give me picture menus. Each day I would point to a different soup and each day various fisheyes, rodent skeletons, and other unidentifiable edibles would rise to the surface for consumption.

In Bangkok, meals were served upon lazy susans. You'd spin your wheel of fortune, stab a food item with your chopsticks, and enjoy your sustenance. Never mind that the fish dishes were of the entire fish, but presumably they'd been gutted before cooking.

While enjoying my first fried chicken meal with my German host family, I tried to be polite by using knife and fork. My host mother, bless her soul, provided me with life advice, "Michael, people all over the world eat fried chicken with their hands."

When my daughter and I were in Rwanda, we visited her host family. Upon arrival, they were proud to show us their new goat staked in the front yard. We were invited back a few days later for the Easter observance. Everyone celebrated except for the goat.

When we took our daughter to Germany, after many years of lapsing language knowledge, my wife ordered us an appetizer of pork. Funny looking pork came in shells that looked a lot like snails. Schenken, Schnecken what's the difference? At least I like gross, slimy things.


The only thing better than raw octopus, eel, and sea urchin on your sushi are chocolate covered centipedes and cockroaches. Protein for all!

# Let's Talk About Things That Go Boom

I was out of town on a manual labor job while in college and volunteered nights ushering at the local college theater. I'm sure the show was good, but night after night we got bomb threats a few hours before showtime. Lacking bomb sniffing dogs and being short on staffing, the police had us, the ushers and other employees, search the premises for signs of bombs.

Let's face it, I was a stoned teenager who wouldn't know what a bomb looked like unless you showed me two sticks of dynamite and a timer. I looked everywhere, except the catwalks. Someone else with a death wish got that horrible duty. Nothing was found.

On the fourth or fifth night, an arriving patron of the arts approached my aisle area carrying a shoe box. As trained, I said, "May I please look inside your box?"

He responded, "No."

My training did not cover what to do next being we were in Iowa, a nice country and all.

"Uh, seriously, sir, I, uh, need to see what you are carrying."

"No."

My training did cover the part that under no circumstances we were to utter the word bomb or threat to the patrons. I guess they wanted them to all die fully unaware of the cause of death.

"I can't let you in unless I know what is in the box, sir."

"No."

"I need to take you to security then, sir."

"No, I am here to see the play."

"You will, sir, just as soon as you talk to security."

He finally relented and I led him to security, leaving my post completely unmanned so that other bomb carrying fiends could blow up the place.

Upon revealing what was in the shoebox I can only say, "Why would an adult man be embarrassed about showing me a shoebox filled with dominoes?" I don't think they were painted C-4 and I didn't see any wires attached to them or anything and the place didn't blow up. Thank goodness for good training.

Once upon a time I helped with fireworks shows. This was before it was automated with switches and remote detonators. In those days, you carried your own canister (calling it an explosive would have been so wrong) and when given the proper command you took it to your designated tube in the ground, inserted it into said tube, then ran like hell before the fire starter could send you into outer space with the glittery mess of lights and the accompanying ooh's and ahh's of the audience, all right before little body parts that used to be you rained down on them.

Anyway, we were told (I won't use the word trained for that as it would make this seem like a righteous operation) that if something were to ever go wrong, it was our duty to mankind, but not personal personhood, to cover our explosive device (I mean canister) with our body. The fatter you were, the better for both sound suppression and splatter material. The key phrase was "fire in the hole." If you were anywhere near the fire starter, with a canister in hand, and heard that death sentence pronounced, then lay atop your own burial pyre.

After the one time it happened to me, I quit on the spot and went home to change my pants and underwear.

Here's the original post, "If you know where I am today, don't worry, I am safe. Sorry to be cryptic, but I don't want to feed the crazies."

The next day, I was able to follow-up with this, "The campus I was on received a bomb threat shortly after noon which led to an evacuation and closure of the campus for the remainder of the day. It looks like it will be business as usual tomorrow for them; however, with missing half my appointments due to the necessary closure, it will not be business as usual for me. Please send your wings and prayers as I need to deliver what they expect with half the knowledge I'm supposed to have."

Here's the whole story, a colleague and I were to have a series of meetings that one might call the discovery type on day one. On day two, we were then to deliver our observations and recommendations. Over lunch on day one we were meeting with the vice president of student affairs while sitting in an elementary classroom when someone came in and whispered in her ear, ala President Bush II on 9/11 . She excused herself briefly, returned even more briefly before receiving another message and then departed without comment or explanation.+

My colleague and I finished our finely catered meals by Subway, discussed the morning's meetings, and prepared for the meetings to come in the afternoon. Only no one showed up for the next meeting or the one following and no one was to be found in the nearby offices.

After an hour or so, being the smart, white collared, highly educated individuals that we are, we surmised that something was amiss. That amiss something had the look of what we always feared technology would turn humans into. Zombieland. Every single person on campus was silently walking while staring at their cell phone. Not a single word was spoken, the church bells all were broken. It was as eerie as the song about the day the music died.

We saw the stream of cars departing campus before we were able to rouse a person from their screen to tell us that a notification for evacuation had just been given due to a canister, er explosives, threat. We joined that line of cars and put together a make-believe presentation for an audience that we weren't sure would be allowed to view it (this was long before the Days of Doom, I mean Zoom).

# The Rookies

We've all been there. Our first solo flight, train ride, trip on a bus, etc. We know we're ignorant, but we can't show our vulnerability to others. Especially us men. Ask for directions? No way. Ask for help of any kind? Not a chance.

I usually see a rookie mistake per trip. What follows happened all in one day, a trip from Omaha to Detroit, just 75 minutes in the air. Easy peasy.

I'd been bumped, free of charge, to first class. On this regional jet that meant 4 square centimeters of extra room and a wider arm rest. I still had to drink my beer out of the can.

As my kind of flying people were called forward to board, there was a little old man two ahead of me in line. Little, as in he made jockeys look big. Tiny as in 4'6" and 75 pounds if we sprayed him down with leaded water. He might not have spoken English or any language as far as I could tell. He'd been delivered by a skycap to the boarding area about an hour ago, his cane a testimony to his mobility issues.

Instead of handing the gate agent his boarding pass, he handed him an ID card of some sort. Instead of asking for his boarding pass, the agent attempted to look him up by name on the computer and came up empty, saying, "You're not on this flight." Language barriers ensued. Finally, a paper boarding pass emerged from his front pocket, and he was cleared to go.

I followed him onto the plane where he promptly sat in seat 1-A. Good for you, man, good for you. I was stuck watching my seatmate in 4-B attempt to fit a loaf of bread into a toaster. I've gone to Asia for two weeks with a suitcase of lesser size. How the gate agent didn't make him check it planeside is a mystery as much as not initially requiring a boarding pass from the old man.

Finally, he conceded that large objects don't fit in small spaces and began to sit down when I said (mind you I'd been watching him for 3-4 minutes from a distance of three feet), "Uh, please don't sit down because I have to crawl into the window seat." He looked at me with confusion, sat down, and placed his bag on his lap where it towered above his sightline.

I tapped him in on the shoulder, pointed at the empty seat beside him, and gestured that my body was to be placed in that location if he would just stand up, get the heck out of the way, and allow the cork he'd placed in the plane aisle to be removed. I guess he understood sign language better than carry-on instructions, because I did get to sit down and wait.

It wasn't long before the rightful renter of seat 1-A found a kind, little man sitting in her seat. More sign language followed as a variety of individuals tried to illustrate to him that his seat numbers below the overhead bins corresponded with two figures on his newly discovered boarding pass. A nice lady led him into the bowels of the plane, presumably to his assigned seat, because we finally pushed back from the gate.

Something about weather in Detroit or Las Vegas, birds pooping on statues in downtown Boston, or some mechanical doohickey needing a tweak meant we got to sit in nice tarmac air conditioning for several minutes. It was just enough time for my seatmate to tell me over and over again that his carry-on had fit on the exact same sized plane a few days ago. I said something like, "Yeah, but that was before you placed all those dead body parts in it."

We flew and landed without issue, albeit several minutes late, and began the deboarding process. For those of you who check your bags planeside, you know the routine. Stand to one side to allow other, luckier, passengers to go on their way while you wait for the second coming of Christ or snow in Hell, whichever comes first.

Of course, no one follows directions, and every passenger is more important than the next. They line both sides of the jet bridge, crowd around the door where bags will appear next week and become increasingly anxious about missed connections over which they have no control.

There I stood, about third in line, which meant my bag would be the last to appear and I'd be trampled to death by then anyway, so who would care? A man of retirement age and teenage temperament stopped in the gaping mouth of the plane door and with a booming voice hollered, "Where is my bag?" The kind flight attendant informed him it was just a few feet beyond. He walked those precious feet, saw that there was no bag, must not have noticed a whole line of innocent bystanders waiting for their bags, and screamed more loudly back toward the plane, "My bag isn't here!!!!"

About twenty of his fellow passengers gently and kindly informed him that his bag would appear in a few minutes and that he should perhaps go to the end of the line and wait patiently like the rest of them. What followed was a slew of frustration about being late to his connection, his geriatric wife about to give birth to a baby penguin, and that it was highway robbery he'd paid $8 for his in-flight Miller Lite.

Finally, we returned to the norm of waiting for death to come before our luggage. One of the final men on the plane to de-board emerged, saw the line and asked me, "Is this the line for bags or are you waiting to get on the plane?"

I took a group from the office on a plane trip for a training. It was going to be great fun until the novice in the group left her pocketbook in the departing airport and remembered it at about 37,000 feet.

Airports frown on not having proper identification. That is why I'm now part of the facial recognition program. Don't worry, you're part of it, too, even if you don't know it.

My first time skiing in the foothills of the Alps—that woman who would later become my wife tried and failed to get the concept that it is a lot drier and warmer if you spend more time upright than laying in the snow.

This was before the prescribing of flying pills, so my patience was low. She'd make it about 100 feet and fall down. After several of these episodes, we worked out a routine: she'd fall down and I'd ski down the mountain, take the chairlift back up, then ski down to her, finding her exactly where I'd left her.

After several weeks, we got to the bottom, I wrestled her into the chair lift, rode to the top, pushed her off her seat, got yelled at by the lift attendant for her impeding the continued rotation of the chairs because she fell down in front of ours.

I took off her skis, walked her to the lodge, bought her a hot toddy and went back to skiing.

At the top of the lift, I looked out and saw fresh powder. Why had no one skied this section yet? Yeah, that thought never entered my addled brain. Off I went.

It was a strange feeling when I got to the bottom and there was nary a chairlift to be seen. Hmmm, I couldn't have skied down the wrong side of the mountain, could I? You know the answer.

In those comfortable walking shoes called ski boots I walked the length of Austria before I found civilization in the form of my beloved sitting warm and dry in front of the fire.

Rookies, you gotta love 'em.

# Things With Wheels

My very first car was a 1969 Ford Maverick, robin egg blue, three on the tree. During that time in my life, I watched the Dukes of Hazzard. So, I knew how to drive and fix cars. That knowledge came in handy.

My buddy and I, having completed our first years of college with Bs in the classroom and straight A's in the bars, took a week-long camping trip in northeast Iowa where they stocked trout streams. Our balanced diet consisted of corn on the cob cooked with butter and wrapped in tin foil thrown into the fire, trout (also with butter and tin foil in the fire), and Old Style beer. I still pity those campground outhouses for the abuse they took.

One pleasant day, we noticed that a trout stream ran over the road. What would Luke Duke do? I backed up many yards, hit the accelerator, skipped second gear on my way from first to third, and stalled out in the middle of the trout stream. I'm sure the DNR would have given me a medal for adding oil and gas to the pristine waters had they learned of my adventure. But, now what to do?

I'd heard the Duke boys talk about a distributor cap and its need to stay dry. I wondered if this thing was the distributor cap. Looks right. Don't have a towel but have a shirt. Wonder if that is dry enough? Well, I'll be damned, it worked. It is a good thing there were rusted holes in the floor because the water drained right out, and we no longer had empty beer cans floating in the backseat.

This day's drive should have been easy; just 3.5 hours across the flatlands. Winds were steady from the south at 40 mph with gusts taking plenty of topsoil to Canada. My canvas truck bed topper was held down in clamps at the tailgate and by Velcro on the sides. Wind is stronger than Velcro. After several stops to re-adhere the Velcro sides, the wind won, breaking metal and plastic alike, releasing seven feet of flying, flapping shrapnel to assault the truck. The canvas held closest to the cab meaning the assault was sustained until I could get stopped. What to do? I had neither the tools nor the know-how to remove the canvas, but I had a steak knife (no idea why that was in the truck). Ended up cutting it free and stuffing it in the cab.

Everyone gets a flat tire every now and then from a stray nail, screw, or chicken bone dropped by a crow. Not me, I'm the guy who buys four new tires on a late Sunday afternoon, parks the car in the garage for the night and discovers all four are flat in the morning (with five minutes to make it to work on time) because they forgot to use any sealant during installation.

I'm the guy, before he started taking flying pills, which got a little, uh, tense when the person resembling my wife failed to provide proper navigation for the eighth time in twenty minutes, thus leading this guy to angrily pull into a parking lot a little too fast and jamming the tire into one of those concrete, park it right here thingies

.

My wife said, "Bring the daughter, her friend and yourself on over to Ireland and meet me in Sneem. It's only a couple hours from Dublin."

What did I know? It takes me that long to drive to my nearest airport out here in the heartland. So, up and over the pound we go, clear customs, move briskly through the rental car selection process, take possession of the keys, and hop right into the car. Except there was no steering wheel. Well, there was a steering wheel, but it was on the wrong side of the car.

Okay, I told myself, I can do this, so I plugged in the GPS (yes, it had an Irish accent), and determined it must be malfunctioning because my two-hour trip is now four. The kids with their fancy smartphones did some interweb, googly eye stuff to confirm that the GPS is accurate. Having now been awake for around twenty-four hours, what could go wrong?

The interstate was easy enough and with navigators covering both sides of the car, we managed the funny driving rules relatively well, until we left modern society's niceties of wide lanes, lane markings, and rest stops.

The concept of shoulders on a road is lost to rural Ireland. Instead of a shoulder, they have rocky cliffs and rock cuts. The first two times I dropped the left side off the road, we bounced right back without a problem. I managed to avoid hitting or being head butted by the sheep that seemed to have the right of way. I even kept the car on the road when tour buses the size of semis with an oversized load warning passed us. I did so by making the girls lean out the car windows furthest away from the cliff drop-off while putting the car onto two wheels. Fun times.

With just fifteen minutes to go in the trip, I hit my third rock. I guess in cricket you only get three strikes. Remember, I said that there are no shoulders in rural Ireland where the roads are narrower than bike lanes? Yeah, that was fun finding enough room to jack up the car.

As I attempted to change the tire without being eaten by a sheep, a kind motorist inquired of needed assistance. We asked them to stop at the hotel where the wife was staying and ask that they bring Guinness or Jameson. I needed all the help I could get.

The kind motorist, also not of the local land, did as directed but was unable to remember from which direction he had arrived at the hotel. Given a fifty-fifty chance of getting it right, my wife and the hotel proprietor jumped into his Porsche and went in search of us….in the wrong direction. By the time they got back to the hotel, I had changed the tire, gotten us to our destination and was becoming good friends with Guinness.

Back in the Adirondacks on a stormy, spring night. For some reason I hadn't yet learned to take a rental car and was driving my personal Jaguar X-Type (okay, kind of a Jag knock off, but I thought I was cool).

I had a mountain on my right and a lake on my left. They don't have shoulders in the Adirondacks either. Typically, it was a fun, winding drive with the Jag.

It was a starless night with steady, light rain when I came around a turn and saw Bigfoot in the middle of the road. With nowhere to swerve, I followed the instructions of my old driver's ed teacher and took it head on.

Blood, guts, and brain matter splashed everywhere. The front axle snapped in two which dropped the car dead in its tracks. Both front tires were flat. I counted fingers, toes, and ribs. All seemed to be in order, so I got out of the car to check on the Yeti.

It turned out that I'd hit a 400-pound rock and ice boulder instead. Probably better for the insurance claim that way.

No cell service, of course, so I waited for a passing motorist to come along with promises to send help once he got a signal. He did better than the Good Samaritan in Ireland.

A service truck arrived alongside a state trooper. The trooper asked if I needed medical attention. I asked that they take my car to the ER instead. The service truck had a special apparatus like the arcade claw game that picked up the larger pieces of the Abominable Snowman and threw them over the side of the road.

A tow truck arrived, and we boogied into town. I expected my insurance company to total the vehicle, but they thought it more economically prudent to tow it five hours to my home location and pay a mechanic to fix it over the span of ten weeks. He got to re-fix it about twenty times, too, over the span of the next year. Lucky me.


I once (ONCE) called my parents for a ride home, because I'd consumed too many liquid hot dogs at the golf course. I'd won some serious prize money and thought it wise to spend all my earnings on my fellow golfers' livers, not to mention my own.

My parents always said that if inebriated, I should call and they'd pick me up, no questions asked.

As I attempted to store their golf cart into the barn erected for such storage, a huge gust of wind bellowed right as two tires blew up, putting the machine up on two wheels. No, I wasn't going too fast downhill while trying to make a ninety-degree turn.

My parents arrived and I climbed into the back seat of my car while my mom got behind the wheel. She asked, "Why are you sitting in the back?"

I answered, "Where will dad sit? Plus, you said there would be no questions."

"Your dad is driving our car back home. Now, why don't you sit up front?"

"I don't understand and that was question number two."

I woke up the next morning on the family room floor, but no questions were asked.

# Four Pheasant and a Fish

In Iowa, ditch chickens, aka pheasant, are often found in ... you guessed it, ditches. It's a lazy man's approach to hunting. You simply drive slowly down the miles of gravel roads hoping the colorful bird is unlucky enough to raise its head during the one-second time span you pass by and are looking in its general direction. After spotting the bird, the lazy hunter must cruise on past a fair distance, quietly exit the vehicle, load the gun, then stealthily approach near enough before the bird flies to get off a shot or two. Ask any road hunter and you'll get a variety of opinions as to the best way to approach a bird in the ditch. I have my own secrets.

The First Bird

The ditches were largely filled with snow and not much cover remained for the birds in which to hide. This usually meant your chances of sneaking up on them were few. I was with a friend, who was driving, when we spotted a rooster huddled up next to a telephone pole. As experienced ditch chicken pursuers we coasted on by for a hundred yards.

We ran through the options and landed on one that is probably not DNR approved. The bird would sit there as long as we didn't draw attention to it or make it feel threatened. It was not bothered by us simply driving by. So, the chosen strategy was for him to drive the car and I was to jog along beside it with the car in between me and the ditch. Once I was in front of the telephone pole, I would stop, the car would roll on by, and the pheasant would die.

I loaded my gun with three shells (hope for the best and plan for the worst) standing on the road while my friend turned the car around. Driving and jogging ensued. The plan worked to perfection. The bird rose into the air, I drew my bead, pulled the trigger, and missed.

A second rooster blasted skyward, taking my attention away from the flying first. Rinse and repeat.

A third rooster followed his brothers with the same result. Perhaps I got shampoo in my eyes. Out of shells and no birds.

The Second Bird

As a traveling salesman in the fall, I had the opportunity to road hunt between appointments that were conveniently scheduled with enough time in between to support my fall habit. On the day in question, I was training a new co-worker who was also a hunter.

Given the tale of The First Pheasant you might understand that my expectations of success are never very high. But on this given day, with something to prove to the new guy, we had plenty of opportunities and success. With five birds dead and needing just one more for our limit, I spotted a ditch chicken right before the end of legal shooting hours.

As I recall, I was wearing a tan sport jacket with a faux, camel hair look to it, brown slacks, probably black shoes, and a narrow striped tie fitting of the era. The bird jumped right in front of me, and I splashed him into a cut corn field where he promptly landed, righted himself, and started running down a row of ankle high stalks. I managed to climb over the barbed wire fence without damage to my nylon pants, arrived at the desired row, and began my chase. As I neared the tiring bird, it jumped two rows over and reversed course. This happened four times. While the bird had to be losing blood, I was losing blood pressure. All the while, my co-worker was standing by the side of the road watching.

Finally, as I neared the bird for the fifth time, I removed my suit jacket, resolved to throw it over the bird before it could jump the rows again. From the gravel I heard, "Don't do it!" followed by roars of laughter. Alas, the bird rolled over sparing me further misery and humiliation.

But that wasn't the end of the story. We had six birds to clean and no tools with which to do so. Upon checking into the Super 8, which was upscale for us in the day, we asked about the possibility of a sharp knife. The kind clerk, being familiar with bird hunters, told us that there were two sawhorses supporting a plywood sheet "out back" and gave us a carpet cutter. So, we did what had to be done but not as efficiently as one might.

Birds now cleaned and meat at the ready, we had another problem. There was no refrigeration. So, for the next three days, those birds rode inside their Ziplock bags in a styrofoam cooler filled with ice (replenished as necessary) that sat in my backseat.

Good times in Iowa.


## The Third Bird

The week after the Super 8 trip, I was riding solo and just two miles from my next stop with 30 minutes to kill, er waste. Back to the gravel and the traveling gun.

In no time, I saw a rooster in the ditch. I did then what I still do today—loaded three shells. Assume I was wearing the same outfit as the cornfield chase episode because there is a 20% chance that I was. Assume I was in the same rental car, probably a Ford Fusion or some other similar marvel of semi-American manufacturing. All the gravel roads look the same, so you don't have to use your imagination.

Keeping on the roll started a week earlier. I hit the first bird, but before I could retrieve it a second rooster appeared and met the same hail of pellets. I had just accomplished my first double. I was excited, thrilled even.

Turning back to the first grounded bird, as I approached it jumped up, ran across the road and through the fence into another cut corn field. I shot again, missed, and watched him scamper away to become coyote food.

Alas, there was still a bird on the ground, so I went to bag my prize only to watch it jump into the air, flap its mighty wings, and give me the middle finger. How many shells did I load? How many shots had I already taken? You know the answer. I would have missed him anyway.

The Fourth Pheasant

Finn, my seven-year-old English Setter, and I returned to our small, northwest Iowa home with three roosters in the bed of my truck: our first limit of the season. Only two of those birds made it to the dinner table.

Finn is a pretty good, but not a great hunter, mostly due to his owner being kind of lazy. His owner is overweight, out of shape, and not a good shot. On December 14, 2021, we ventured out expecting little. A five-inch snow had fallen four days prior, and we'd tried the last two days unsuccessfully to find any birds, now perplexed as to where they had gone.

Just minutes into the hunt, Finn held steady as a rooster bolted up from the draw. One shot had him on the ground just twenty yards away. Dumb bird flew in the direction I was pointing the gun. Finn was on him in a flash of slobbering non-retrieval. Bagging the bird, we marched on, jumping seven hens, the majority of which busted at my feet. Finn pointed to some of them.

The adjacent draw is skinny on good days and anorexic after snowfalls. Finn, as he and his breed are apt to do, raced ahead showing the "all clear of birds" sign as he ran. I plodded well behind hoping he'd get to the end and come back, saving me steps. I was sweating and my glasses were fogging even though I'd turned my fluorescent orange hat backwards.

He got to the end but didn't turn around. The receiver I carry for his GPS collar beeped indicating he'd stopped. I say stopped instead of pointed because he stop-points a lot. Sometimes he's right; often he's not. Yet, I've learned that the moment I quit trusting him the bird wins – so on I trudged through the soggy snow—he was 256 yards from me.

True to normal form, as I approached, he broke, leapt ten yards ahead and turned into a dog statue. I looked to my right and saw the tracks. Walking slowly, I saw the tracks disappear into the meagerest of cover. One deep breath to ready myself before the bird sailed out. I rushed the first shot, missed, re-grouped, and dropped him to the ground.

Where he bounced and started running for the next county. Finn was in hot pursuit. I watched the two fighter jets mirror the other's move for three minutes before another slobber bath was administered as punishment. I retrieved our collective prize, and we made our way back to the truck, one of us done walking for the day. We took pictures of Finn and the two birds on the tailgate.

As is our custom, we took the gravel roads back to town. Having traveled but a mile, I spotted a rooster hiding under a little pine tree in a ditch. Irritating Finn, I got out alone, walked toward the tree and completed my limit as it unsuccessfully attempted escape. Three birds, four shells, fifty minutes. We'd never done better.

Leaving Finn in the cab of the truck when we arrived home, I got out to arrange the birds on the tailgate for the obligatory picture. Opening the tailgate, I saw two dead pheasants and blood everywhere. That last bird, a big, spurred holdover of at least a year, was running around the bed. I rolled back the top and grabbed the damned thing. All I got was every butt and tail feather to his name.

He jumped from the truck, screamed down the driveway, hooked left and was gone. I tried to follow but soon lost him. Finn, once leashed, couldn't pick up the trail again.

So, if you're in Storm Lake, Iowa and see a big, proud rooster without tail feathers, just let him be. He's earned his freedom.

## The Fish

I didn't just hunt in between sales calls; I also carried a fishing pole and tackle box. In Iowa Falls, Iowa there runs a river through the idyllic, small town called, improbably, the Iowa River. In the middle of the town there is a dam. Fish like dams. Big fish like big dams. This was a big dam.

I often caught smallish crappie and other assorted panfish. No big deal handling small fish while clad in your Sunday best. This time though, I tied into a lunker. I can still hear the drag of the reel screaming as I fought the fish and the current off the dam. Rivers are murky so you never know exactly what you have until it breaks the surface quite near to you. Did I have a big catfish, perhaps a rare sturgeon?

Finally, just below my dress shoes, it surfaced like a submarine. This was a ten-pound northern pike. Probably pushing three feet. All fish smell, but northerns are particularly hard on the olfactory. I still had a sales call to make. If I landed that fish by hand (I had no net because my expectations were never that high), it would thrash and splash and make me unpresentable to paying customers. What to do?

I could cut the line but losing that $5 lure was more than my pocketbook and ego could stand. Could I walk it far enough downstream to pull it onto the bank and drag it toward the car without touching it? I'm sure I had a towel or something there to wrap it in until I could find another carpet knife at the Super 8. Probably not in dress clothes and the muddy shore. The easy answer would have been to carry a pair of pliers and just pull the lure from the mouth without the fish ever leaving the water. I didn't need to eat it anyway. Yeah, I didn't have any pliers in the tackle box, which was still in the car anyway because I was only going to make 5-10 casts.

Ultimately, the decision was made for me. The fish rolled over, spit the hook and went back to the dam. Damn, that's why you don't see a picture about this great (near) catch. Fishermen never lie.

Bonus Story

I was a novice turkey hunter in unfamiliar woods in northeastern Pennsylvania. I'd read Stephen King's book "The Girl Who Loved Tom Gordon," about a young girl lost in the woods. When lost in the woods you are to sit your butt down and wait for someone to rescue you.

That works really well if your loved ones, or anyone, know where you are generally going to be. As you've figured out by now, I'm not that smart.

I walked in circles. I petted rattlesnakes that looked like sticks. I ate dandelions and drank from streams. I was getting scared after just 30 minutes.

At some point I ended up on an unnamed road. I flipped a coin and turned right. Understand, I'm in full camo, with face protection, and I'm carrying a gun.

At long last I came upon a settlement, but no pioneers were in sight. Toward the end of the village a lass was hanging clothes onto her line in her backyard. I gently laid my gun on the ground and approached while making some noise so as not to startle her.

She was kind enough not to call her redneck husband to arms, pointed me in the right direction, and off I went to the knoll overlooking my hunting grounds.

Scanning my decoys from two hundred yards away, there was a fox sitting where one decoy had been. The fox and I both had disappointing days.

# Noises and Things in The Air

Sometimes it feels like I'm the only one who notices things or maybe I'm the only one on board who thinks he's in imminent danger of immediate and fiery death. I give you these examples:

When the cockpit door is open and you're parked at the gate before take-off, I often hear a mechanical voice demand, sometimes frequently, "Roll Call!!"

In the early years I would often respond, "Seat 4B, here!" People looked at me funny. I still don't understand because when Mrs. Blutarsky took roll call in second grade she'd say, "Mike Frantz," and I'd say, "Here."

It is not uncommon for me to hear what sounds like an alarm coming from the cockpit while we are in flight. Often it is three blasts from what sounds like an air raid warning, except I have nowhere to hide. No one else seems to be concerned. Is it a warning alerting the pilots that they are about to stall out, that the top of the mountain is two inches from the belly of the plane, that a flock of pythons has just rendered the engines inoperable? I never get an explanation.

I've had ice form and dangle from the panels above me where my precious oxygen laden bag that doesn't fully inflate resides. That can't be good. I mean, they de-ice the exterior of the plane for safety reasons. Shouldn't they do the same inside? What would happen if so much ice formed that the plane got to be too heavy to fly? That all sounds dangerous.

I've also had water drip from the panel above me. There are wires and electrical things up there. I've seen them when the panels are broken. Daddy taught me at an early age not to drop the hair dryer, hair curler, or bread toaster into the bathtub unless they were unplugged. Water and electricity don't mix so why are they allowed inside a metal tube hurtling through the air by magic alone?

Then, there are the noises that come from below my feet. Sure, sometimes it is just the landing gear being deployed, but that doesn't happen at cruising altitude, does it? Did the pet buffalo just escape from its cage in the cargo hold? Is the Unabomber hiding out in the wheel well? I never get a good explanation.

Why doesn't anyone else think about these things? Am I really just that paranoid?

Flight Attendants' Instructions

I know you don't listen to their instructions because you think you have them memorized. We've all seen the humorous videos of flight attendants bringing these mundane announcements to life through humor, song, dance, and improv on the tarmac. Yeah, I've never witnessed any of them outside of YouTube.

So, why do they tell us how to insert the nose of one side into the mouth of the other? Sticking your nose into another's mouth is kind of gross, I suspect. Plus, it has to be the easiest thing in the world to figure out on your own. So, why do they do it?

Because some litigious idiot somewhere didn't buckle up and got thrown into the ceiling during heavy turbulence that was previously forecast, via loudspeaker announcement by the pilot, and then sued and won against the airline.

The flight attendants tell us not to worry if the oxygen bag doesn't fully inflate, because oxygen is still flowing. Why? Because some jackoff panicked during an air decompression incident and then sued the airline for not telling him that he shouldn't panic during the scariest freaking moment of his life.

They tell us that baby life jackets are available upon request and that, often, an extra life raft like the baby life jackets are in overhead compartments. Has anyone ever verified this? What if we asked for proof? That's right, nobody has sued over that …. yet.

Why do they announce that removing or damaging smoke detectors in the lavatory is punishable by law? Why do they call it a lavatory instead of a bathroom? But I digress. They tell us because some Mensa member did just that in order to have a smoke in flight. He probably didn't have to pay a fine because once upon a time, they didn't make that a part of their announcement regimen.

The pandemic added another announcement. Even though the flight attendants are wearing masks during the safety demonstration for their safety and yours, please remove your lifesaving mask before putting on the airplane's lifesaving oxygen mask. By now, you can guess why they have to state the obvious. Damn lawyers.

It won't be long before the pre-flight announcements are longer than the flights because of idiots who think they have a right under the Second Amendment to bear arms inside a flying casket full of live people.

# The Big Finale

My wife and I were about to return to the good old U S of A, but we had to get a negative COVID test before being allowed back into the country that didn't believe there had ever been a worldwide pandemic. You remember, the vaccines caused windmills to alter your DNA because we didn't inject bleach into the hurricanes to prevent them from swallowing New Orleans. At least that's what I heard on the unbiased news stations.

So, we caught a cab to this place labeled "ROCDOC." I have no idea what that meant, but there were something like 50 unoccupied stalls and several people in full hazmat suits walking around. We were the only patients, and once our cab departed, there were no other cars in the parking lot. Not a great business model I suspect.

Anyways, this nice, young man who was about to board the space shuttle for Pluto led us into one stall, confirmed our identities and testing intentions, and told me to, "Tilt your head back, I don't have to put the swab in very far, and relax."

He then produced a mop, climbed onto the chair adjacent to me, raised the mop, two-handed over his head, and jammed it first into one nostril, then the other. "See, that wasn't so bad." You'll have the result emailed to you in an hour. He then took a teeny tiny toothpick sized swab and tested my wife.

We got back to the hotel, had some dinner, got our emails that we were negative for cooties, then emails from the airline telling us that my wife's birth date didn't match her test results and that my test was not negative. Given the hour, there was nothing to be done, no arguments to be made to anyone, no corrective action available.

In the morning, we arrived at the airport in trepidation and with evidence of our negative tests on our phones. The baggage check agent took our passports, gave us boarding passes, and checked in our luggage without comment.

Next stop, in-country customs and security. Take your belt off but keep your shoes on. Put all carry-on items into bins, grab your butt, promenade through the x-ray machine, and hope you don't end up in a North Korean prison.

Now, on to the American customs and security line while still not on American soil. Take your shoes off, keep your belt on, don't put your personal items into bins, pray for rain on the prairie, and hope they don't make you recite the Gettysburg address.

Somewhere in the prior ten hours our birth date and test issues were resolved by artificial intelligence or Big Brother or Mickey Mouse. Our reward was to wait in the international terminal that had one seat for every ten passengers. Something to do with social distancing where they could control how many seats there were, and it was better to have a crowd standing shoulder to shoulder rather than sitting cheek to cheek. Whatever.

We returned home safely and thirty-one hours after arrival I was back in my truck heading to the same airport but with a work destination ahead. My wife and I had hardly been separated by more than a few feet for an entire week. We'd dined and slept together, sat next to each other on trains, planes and automobiles. In short, we sucked all the same air.

My plane landed, I got my rental car, and was thirty minutes from my final destination when she called, "I have bad news, I tested positive."

"You mean, the airline finally called you?"

"No."

"ROCDOC made a mistake?"

"No."

"You stood in front of that windmill again, didn't you?"

"No, my throat was scratchy, so I took an in-home test."

So, there I was, one thousand miles from home, unable to assist my ill wife, unable to return home for fear of infection (if not already doomed), with four days of clothes for what would now be an eleven day trip. Never mind I was wearing the only pair of shorts and t-shirt I brought, and the temperatures were forecast for the nineties. A small price to pay given my wife's condition.

I had to buy my own testing mops and report my findings to myself while isolating in a little apartment in a faraway state. Good times.

I'm telling you, don't travel with Mike. Something bad is going to happen. The victim might just be you.


I don't Twitter or Tweet or Twerk, but maybe we can start a thread, a strand, or a trend. I'd like to see how many false reports of me there are across the globe:

#donttravelwithmike

# Meet the Author

Mike is the best-selling author of many books that have never been published. His humor has not appeared on any late shows, and he is usually the life of no parties. He could be you but be glad that isn't the case. If you tell yourself that you could do what he has done, then you would be right. But you didn't and now you're reading about him instead of you.

The amazing thing about the author, Michael Frantz, is that there is nothing special about the author, Michael Frantz. He is just another middle-aged, middle-class, balding guy whose looks are forgotten as soon as you glance past him. He married the woman whom he first rejected due to her lack of sobriety. They have adult children in D.C. and Toronto, all of whom are far enough away from their home in Storm Lake, Iowa, to consider themselves clear of the dark cloud hanging over their dad. Storm Lake is a place many miles from rental car agencies, bus stops, train stations, and airports. There is a reason he has been ordered to live there yet travel for his job.

You can find more at:
Mikefrantz.substack.com

www.ingramcontent.com/pod-product-compliance
Lightning Source LLC
Chambersburg PA
CBHW042126100526
44587CB00026B/4192